Cryptocurrency

Everything You Should Know About Cryptocurrency From Beginner To Advanced

Table of Contents

INTRODUCTION 5

CHAPTER 1 – WHAT IS CRYPTOCURRENCY AND HOW DOES IT WORK? 7

    WHAT ARE CRYPTOCURRENCIES? 7
    A SHORT HISTORY OF CRYPTOCURRENCIES 8
    CRYPTOCURRENCY AS A MEDIUM OF EXCHANGE 11

CHAPTER 2 – THE TECHNOLOGY UNDER THE HOOD 14

    WHAT IS THE BLOCKCHAIN TECHNOLOGY? 14
    IMPORTANT CONCEPTS: 14
    THE REWARD 20
    MINING NETWORKS (MINING POOLS) 20
    BLOCKCHAIN FORK 21
    THERE ARE TWO TYPES OF FORK IN THE SYSTEM: 22
    THE DAO HACK 23

CHAPTER 3 – HOW DO CRYPTOCURRENCIES AFFECT YOU? 25

    WILL IT BECOME A WIDELY-USED CURRENCY? 25
    ARE YOU CONSIDERING TRADING IT? 26
    WILL IT BE OUTMODED BECAUSE OF OTHER EMERGING TECHNOLOGIES? 29

CHAPTER 4 – HOW TO START WITH CRYPTOCURRENCIES 30

    MINER 30
    CONSUMER/USER 31
    INVESTOR 31
    TRADER 31
    SERVICE PROVIDER 32
    OWNING YOUR FIRST CRYPTO COINS 33
    PRINCIPLES TO FOLLOW TO KEEP YOUR CRYPTOCURRENCY SAFE: 40

CHAPTER 5 – MOST POPULAR CRYPTOCURRENCIES 44

BITCOIN 44
ETHEREUM 45
RIPPLE 47
BITCOIN CASH 49
LITECOIN 50
CARDANO 51

CHAPTER 6 – HOW TO TRADE CRYPTOCURRENCIES 53

UNDERSTANDING CURRENCY PAIRS 53
CRYPTOCURRENCY EXCHANGES 54
MOST SUCCESSFUL CRYPTOCURRENCY EXCHANGES: 58
TRADING STRATEGIES 61
MAKE SURE YOU ARE UP TO THE CHALLENGE 61
OPERATE BIG 61
TRADE SHORT WHEN THE MARKET IS BOOMING 62
DIVERSIFY AS YOUR PORTFOLIO GROWS 63
DO FUNDAMENTAL ANALYSIS OF ALL CRYPTOCURRENCIES YOU TRADE WITH 64
BET ON THE CRYPTOCURRENCY THAT IS LIKELY TO BECOME REAL MONEY 66
LOOK INTO THE PARTICIPATION OF INSTITUTIONAL INVESTORS IN THE CRYPTO MARKET 67
TIME YOUR ENTRY IN THE MARKET 67
USE INDEX INVESTING PRINCIPLES ON PICKING CURRENCIES 69
QUIT WHILE YOU ARE AHEAD 70
BUYING LONGER TERM VERSUS DAY-TRADING 71

CHAPTER 7 – WHY IS THE PRICE SO VOLATILE 73

CRYPTOCURRENCY VERSUS FIAT CURRENCY 73
THE SOCIAL MEDIA CULTURE 76
THE ACTIONS OF TRADERS 78
LACK OF AN INTRINSIC VALUE 80
THE INFLATION RATE OF THE SOURCE COUNTRY OF YOUR OPERATIONAL FIAT CURRENCY 83

CHAPTER 8 – THE DARK SIDE OF THE CRYPTOCURRENCY MARKET 84
- Fake ICOs..84
- Credit Card Scams 85
- Pump and Dump Schemes 86
- Money Laundering 87

CHAPTER 9 – THE CURRENT STATE OF THE MARKET 88
- The Near Future 88
- Positive Government Policies 89
- Integration with other Industries...........................89
- Increased Usage Rate Outside as actual Currencies...........90
- The Distant Future 91

CONCLUSION 92

Introduction

If you are reading this, you have probably already heard about the big cryptocurrency price boom that happened in 2017. If you are like most people who are outside for the cryptocurrency loop, you are probably wondering why it happened. Why is the investing market going gaga over this new technology? Are cryptocurrency and the blockchain (its underlying technology) really the way of the future? Most importantly, how do these emerging technologies affect you?

This book aims to answer these questions for you. It covers the most basic topics like what blockchain is and what cryptocurrencies are. It also talks about the events that happened since the inception of cryptocurrency in the late 90s and 2000's, up until now.

When you are done reading this book, you will have effectively caught up with the things happening in the cryptocurrency market. It discusses the different types of cryptocurrencies and the developmental process that each of them is taking. It talks about the communities that are surrounding this market and how they influence the cryptocurrency world.

This book even talks about the steps that you can take if you want to take part in the cryptocurrency market as a trader, a miner or a user. Knowing the different roles that you can take in the currency market is essential in getting a bird's eye view of the entire industry.

Regardless of what the experts are saying, cryptocurrencies are here to stay. People are rooting for these new forms of currencies to succeed and they are showing their support by investing in them. By learning all about them, you will be able to make an informed decision on whether you want to take part in this industry or not.

Let's begin the journey.

Chapter 1 – What is Cryptocurrency and How does It Work?

Cryptocurrencies like Bitcoin and Ethereum are always in the news. Their popularity comes from the fact that they are now an actively traded asset. Many people are considering taking part in trading these new forms of digital assets. However, most of them are doomed to lose money if they do not do their research first, before taking part in the cryptocurrency market.

In this chapter, we will discuss what these cryptocurrencies are and how they work.

What are Cryptocurrencies?

Cryptocurrencies, as the name suggests, is meant to be a replacement of cash when transacting through the internet. The creators of this new form of cash thought, that because the internet has no borders, there should not be any barriers stopping the transactions between buyers and sellers around the world.

Before cryptocurrencies, online businesses were limited by many factors from becoming truly global. An online business for example, only uses the fiat currency from its country of origin. A business in Japan for example, is likely to use the Japanese Yen to transact. If the business wants to become truly global, it needs to open merchant accounts that accept currencies from different countries.

By doing this, the business is exposing itself to many risks such as the possibility of a disadvantageous exchange rate with other currencies. With currencies from more than a hundred of different countries, it is impossible to keep track of each one.

A successfully established cryptocurrency aims to change all this. By dealing with just a handful of cryptocurrencies, businesses around the world can minimize the currency exchange risk.

A short history of Cryptocurrencies

The idea of an online currency is not new. However, in the past, it has only been explored in the academic field of computer science. In practice however, businesses still prefer using the digital form of fiat currencies when transacting online.

The first publicly announced effort to establish an online currency free from any fiat currency was back in 1983 by a cryptographer named David Chaum. He introduced the virtual currency called eCash which is designed to keep the users anonymous through the use of cryptography. In 1983 however, the number of internet users was still low, not to mention the number of businesses who already operated online. Because of the immaturity of the online business world, the first version of the cryptocurrency did not take off.

In 1996, the US National Security Agency (NSA) published a paper called *"How to Make a Mint: the Cryptography of Anonymous Electronic Cash"*. It talked about the creation of an anonymous electronic currency. It was published in the Massachusetts Institute of Technology (MIT) mailing list and volume 46 of the 1997 issue of The American Law Review.

It was no surprise that the implementation of the concepts discussed in the paper was immediately tested by Wei Dai, a computer engineer and one of the pioneers of the cryptocurrency industry. He published B-Money, which is an electronic cash system similar to the modern day cryptocurrency. The system also used cryptography to keep the identity of the users anonymous. The paper that talked about B-Money was published in 1998.

In the same year, Nick Szabo, a pioneer in the field and also a computer scientist, introduced bitgold, which is an early version of the modern day bitcoin. It is the first electronic currency system that applied the use of "Proof of Work". Szabo also coined the phrase "smart contract" which is one of the central features of cryptocurrencies like Ethereum.

It wasn't until 2008 however, that the biggest cryptocurrency to date was introduced. It started with the registration of the domain name bitcoin.org. In November of the same year, a paper called "Bitcoin: A Peer-to-Peer Electronic Cash System" was released in multiple cryptography mailing lists. The developer implemented the open source bitcoin software in the beginning of 2009.

At the same time, Satoshi Nakamoto, mined the first block in the Bitcoin blockchain with the text:

"The Times 03/Jan/2009 Chancellor on brink of second bailout for banks."

In 2011, the next two cryptocurrencies were developed and implemented. These were Namecoin and Litecoin. This was followed by multiple other cryptocurrencies. Since the introduction of Bitcoin, many cryptocurrencies have been implemented but many of them have also failed.

Bitcoin and other cryptocurrencies began growing their community of miners. The leader of the pack however, has always been Bitcoin, garnering the highest market cap among other cryptocurrencies in the market.

The media attention around cryptocurrencies started to grow at around 2013, when the value of bitcoin began rising. From 2011 to 2012, the value of Bitcoin fluctuated from less than $1 to $17. However, the price began to climb steadily in the later parts of 2012.

2013 was the first break out year for Bitcoin. The cryptocurrency opened the year at around $13 per bitcoin. In just one month, the value of the currency more than doubled to $32. It continued to rise until April, when it breached the $100 mark. With news surrounding the new currency in the market spreading throughout the internet, the price of bitcoin peaked again in just nine days. On April 9, bitcoin prices breached the $200 mark before plummeting back to below $100 four days later.

The stories about bitcoin however, would not end there. In the same year, the price of the cryptocurrency remained below $200. It wasn't until November of that year when bitcoin exceeded all expectations. It climbed back to $200 in November 2, 2013. From there, it continued to rise before the year ended, breaching the $1,000.00 mark on November 30, 2013.

However, with investors taking their share of the profits, the value plummeted back down. The value remained below $500 for in 2014 up to the middle part of 2016. That's when things began to shift again. With the news about bitcoin spreading again, the market value began to rise. Bitcoin ended 2016 priced just below $900. Once it breached the $1,000-mark in March 2017, the price just kept on rising. From there, it rose to a price of more than $17,500 in December 11, 2017.

Together with the rise of bitcoin, other cryptocurrencies also got a lot of attention. Ethereum is the clear second biggest currency behind it. Other newer coins like Cardano and Ripple also benefited in the 2017 boom. Ripple in particular, had a successful ICO partly because of the success that Bitcoin was experiencing.

Just like with what happened in 2013, traders started profit taking in the early part of 2018. The price plummeted back to under $8,000 in February. The price has not recovered to its peak price as of the writing of this book. However, with just under 20% of bitcoin left to mine, the value of bitcoin is expected to rise in the future but investors and traders need to weather through massive price fluctuations before this happens.

The success of bitcoin and other cryptocurrencies however, were only in their function as trading assets and not as actual currencies. Most people who are holding these coins do not necessarily want to spend them as mediums of exchange. Instead, they are mostly used a way to grow investment portfolios

Cryptocurrency as a Medium of Exchange

For a cryptocurrency to become successful in replacing money online however, it first needs a number of important factors to fall in place:

- Stability in price

The biggest factor affecting Bitcoin and other cryptocurrency is the issue with its price volatility. Because it is freely exchanged currency with no central bank to manage it, the prices can be pretty volatile. The prices in one part of the world where trade volumes are high can differ from the prices in other exchanges where trades volume is low. Because of these factors, prices have been fluctuating for thousands of dollars per unit.

If a cryptocurrency is to become a serious medium of exchange, a feature needs to be introduced that will prevent its price from rising or falling by thousands of dollars in a day. This will make it less attractive as an investment asset, but it is necessary to make it work as a true currency.

- A policy consensus among governments

In the wake of the 2017 cryptocurrency boom, governments and their central banks have been looking into how the hype can affect their economies and the financial wellbeing of their people. Governments in countries with high volumes of trades in particular were alarmed by the number of their citizens participating in the trade market.

As a response, these governments took a stand in the early days of 2018. South Korea in particular, had a massive crackdown on local cryptocurrency exchanges for their roles in laundering money. Other countries followed suit in creating new policies in handling cryptocurrency as an investment asset.

These government responses made it clear that the days of unregulated trading are over. This resulted in the massive dip in the prices of the most commonly traded cryptocurrencies. From $17,000, Bitcoin's value dipped to $11,000 in a matter of two days. It even went as far as $7,000 in the following week. This is the first ever massive correction in the price of bitcoin and some of the new cryptocurrencies.

The value of these cryptocurrencies can go back up to its previous high prices but this can only happen if the governments of major economies like China, Japan, the Euro zone, the US and Canada agree on a unified strategy on how to police bitcoin and the other cryptocurrencies.

- An industry to embrace it as a payment method

The different cryptocurrencies in the market today are in a race to becoming accepted as a currency. Some of them are trying to do it by becoming the first cryptocurrency to be widely accepted in a specific industry.

Ethereum for instance, is becoming a popular experimental platform for developers. It will completely take off if developers can successfully create widely used apps and websites run in the Ethereum network. However, none of the startups using Ethereum's smart contracts have broken through the mainstream yet. With thousands of developers working with the platform though, it's just a matter of time before Ethereum can be considered a new internet and Ether as its fiat currency.

Ripple and Litecoin on the other hand, are taking a different approach in breaking out into the mainstream. They are partnering with as many banks and financial institutions as they can to make sure that people have access to their currencies. Ripple was particularly popular in its initial coin offering because of the many connections it already had since the first day of trading. It has partnered with big banks like Standard Chartered and Royal Bank of Canada. Recently, Litecoin has also advanced in partnering with popular money-sending service Western Union. These cryptocurrencies are working with these banks and financial institutions to start building their infrastructure in the financial world. As to how the blockchain technology can be applied in this industry, is yet to be seen. We will need to wait for the services that will come out from these partnerships and see how the market will respond to them.

- Improvements in technology in facilitating transactions

The mining network of a cryptocurrency is its backbone. Not only do they keep the blockchain going by adding transaction blocks to them, miners and miner groups hold some of the biggest cryptocurrency reserves in the world. However, even with all the energy and computing power that goes into the mining of the most popular cryptocurrencies like Bitcoin and Ethereum, the transaction time still lags.

Chapter 2 – The Technology Under the Hood

Now that we know what cryptocurrencies are and how they evolved through the years, let's talk about the technology that all of them have in common, the blockchain.

What is the Blockchain Technology?

The blockchain is the technological breakthrough that makes cryptocurrencies possible. To explain, the blockchain is simply an online ledger that all the people participating in the network of a certain cryptocurrency shares. This ledger contains all the transactions in the history of the cryptocurrency. It uses cryptography and the participation of so many people to ensure that the details of the transaction will never be changed.

Important Concepts:

Online Ledger

The online ledger in a blockchain is just like its offline counterparts. It is merely a list of the transactions or the exchange of the currency from one user to another. In its most basic form, the exchange of a cryptocurrency is detailed in a ledger with the amount exchanged as well as the account numbers of the sender and receiver of the currency.

The Blockchain Use Case

The blockchain is basically just a type of software that a network of computers shares. The computers in the network, through the application of the software, follow the same set of rules. These rules dictate how the users in the network interact and make use of the unique featured programed into the cryptocurrency.

The different activities of the users of the network, their interaction with other users and the overall outcome of these activities are collectively called the "use case". In a cryptocurrency's whitepaper for example, the developers should lay out the user cases that they intend for their technology so that the users will be able to decide what role they will play in it.

The primary use case for bitcoin for example is to become a medium of exchange in the internet. For Ethereum, the primary user case is to support the development of DAPPs.

Transaction Blocks

Inside the online ledger are transaction blocks that are arranged like a chain. The older transaction blocks are placed in the beginning of the chain while the newer are in the front end of the chain. Whenever a new transaction is created, it is added to a pool of transactions.

The miners are responsible for creating blocks. They take a set of transactions from the transaction pool and form them into blocks. They then need to solve a cryptographic puzzle before their block is added to the chain.

Nodes

To make sure that the ledger's integrity is kept, the correct ledger is shared to all the computers in the cryptocurrency network.

These computers are known as nodes. Once a transaction block is created through the mining process of a cryptocurrency, it is added to the chain in the online ledger. When this happens, the updated form of the ledger is then shared to all nodes in the network to let everyone know about the new transactions added to the chain.

The difficulty of creating blocks ensures that no node can send out fake ledgers to unsuspecting nodes. By the time a fraud ledger is sent out, all the other nodes in the network are already way ahead in the blockchain. A node that receives a fake blockchain will simply check the online ledgers of other nodes. This will make it discard the fake ledger and stick to the one that is commonly used by the other nodes.

The Private Key, The Public Key and The Signature

When a person who wants to start using cryptocurrencies sign up with an online wallet account, he or she is given a private and public key. These two keys are probably the most important parts of your cryptocurrency accounts.

To protect the identity of the people transacting, their accounts do not have names. Instead, they are identified through their public key. These keys are merely a set of numbers and letters that represent a person's account in the network. The public keys are generated by passing the private keys through a cryptographic process. A cryptocurrency user can typically generate more public keys because they should only be used for one transaction.

Because there is no real cash or physical coins present, there is no need for a physical account or deposit box. The only way for a person to know how much of a cryptocurrency he or she owns is by going through the history of the blockchain and find all the transactions going in and out of his private key.

Think of the public key as your address where people can send a specific cryptocurrency to. If I want another user to send me their cryptocurrency, I will need to let them know about my public key. They will use my public key to decrypt the details of the transaction. This should include the amount of cryptocurrency sent to my account and the amount deducted from their account.

To authenticate the transaction, another feature is added called the digital signature. Just like in the real world, you will need a signature to let the people know that it is truly you who are sending the money and not some fraudster. When you create a transaction, the software that manages the transaction for you automatically signs it upon confirmation. The signature is merely a hash that can be decoded by the miners. A hash is a long number that is the result of running the private key of the sender through a cryptographic function. The miners and other people who want to confirm the signature can use the public key that comes with the message to decrypt it. This way, they will never have access to the private key of the user.

With cryptocurrencies like bitcoin, there are no financial institutions mediating between users. The people exchanging money can do so by using only their public keys and private keys.

It is important for a user to keep his or her private key safe. Ideally, he or she should be the only person to access this data because it holds the key for making online transactions. If another person knows the private keys to a bitcoin account, that person has the complete freedom to spend all the coins in that account.

Miners

In the real world, we have banks and similar financial institutions that validate out identities to the people we are transacting with. When you send money to someone through their bank account, the bank will ask for the name of the person you are sending the money to and their account number. Without these details, the bank will not be able to go through with the transaction. Ideally, the bank should also inform the other person if a certain amount of money went into their account.

The banks however, ask for a transaction fee as a payment for their service. A person sending money frequently will need to pay multiple transaction fees. Aside from this, they are also bound by the laws of the land where they operate. If a transaction raises a red flag, it may be halted and the accounts may be investigated.

With cryptocurrencies, there are no financial institutions assuring users of the identity of the users at the other and of the line. People who use cryptocurrencies trust the blockchain and its underlying technology to make sure that their transactions are honored and added to the blockchain.

To take the place of the financial institutions, the blockchain has miners. Miners are just people with high computing powers who then lend their computing powers to the system.

The number of miners in the network is one of the safeguards that a cryptocurrency has. Each miner computer serves as a node. It keeps a copy of the updated version of the blockchain.

Aside from this, the miners are also responsible for creating transaction blocks that need to be added to the ledger. As stated earlier, the miners take a set of transactions from the transaction pool. These transactions are organized to create a proposed transaction block. A mining software uses a cryptographic function to code the contents of the transaction blocks. In the case of the bitcoin, the cryptographic function uses is the SHA-256. Each cryptocurrency uses a different hashing function.

Mining however, is not that easy. The more miners there are in a network, the faster it is to generate blocks. This is where the *mining difficulty* comes into play.

Aside from hashing the transaction blocks, the miners need to follow a certain rule that sets the difficulty of creating blocks. In the case of bitcoins, the difficulty is set through the block headers. The header is made up of a 256-bit number. In computer terms, a 256-bit number is a very large number.

For a block to be accepted in the blockchain, its header must be lower than the published target. The target is also 256-bit number that is set by the bitcoin algorithm after every 2016 blocks. If the mining community creates this number of blocks too fast, the target is made more difficult. In the case of the 256-bit number, it is made lower. The target starts with multiple zeros in front of it most of the time. It is extremely difficult for a miner to hash a header for a block with so many zeros in front of it.

Think of it as a probability puzzle. Consider the 256-bit number as a very large number and the target is set very low. For a miner to successfully create a block, he or she needs to create one with a header that is lower than the target. However, the only way to achieve this is to pull a random 256-bit number out. Since the number of possible numbers is extremely high, the odds of getting correct 256-bit number are almost impossible. However, the task is made possible by the number of computers (nodes) in the network. Each of these computers can make at least a hundred of thousands of guesses in a minute. Regardless of the difficulty level, it is just a matter of time for some random computer in the node will be able to make the block.

As of the writing of this book, there are just over 11,000 nodes in the bitcoin network. This does not speak of the computing power in the network though. The number of graphic cards in these computers varies. Some can have as few as 4 cards while other specialized mining rigs can have ten to twenty cards in them.

For miners to create a block with the header hash below the target, they need to use the computing power of their devices. The computer basically runs the hashing function as fast as it could in the hopes of creating a 256-bit number in the header lower than the target. The lower the target is, the lesser the likelihood that this will happen, therefore increasing the difficulty. Given enough time, a computer will eventually get lucky and create a hash that fits the target.

With the number of computers trying to create the next block ever increasing however, the miners are in a race against each other. With the high number of miners, the difficulty of mining in 2018 has increased significantly compared to the targets in 2016, before the sharp increase in the price of coins.

The Reward

The miners in the network are rewarded with cryptocurrency for their efforts. The amount of cryptocurrency that they get varies. In the beginning, bitcoin rewarded as much as 50 coins per block created. The reward however, is set to reduce over time. For bitcoin, the reward is halved after every 210,000 blocks are created. As of the writing of this book, the reward is currently set at 12.5 bitcoins per block mined. It is set to reduce to 6.25 bitcoins per block in the next halving.

With 1,800 bitcoins mined every day, the 210,000 mark will be reached on June 1, 2020.

Mining Networks (Mining Pools)

With mining becoming more popular, massive amounts of computing power is entering the cryptocurrency networks every month. However, many regular people who have smaller computer units are entertaining the thought of taking part in the revolution. Unfortunately for them, the minute computing power that they offer in the network does not stand a chance to compete against the big players who have specialized devices for mining.

This is the problem that gave birth to the concept of mining pools. A mining pool is a bitcoin mining services where in groups of people can combine their computing power so that they will be able to compete against the bigger players. A person planning to mine bitcoin for example, could join the mining pool, install their software and start mining. Instead of each computer mining independently, the mining pool software uses the hashing power offered by each member efficiently. In an ideally coded mining pool software, it will be able to make an efficient attempt to solve the hash puzzle. However, since the codes of each mining pool vary, some of them are more efficient than others.

The members of the pool are rewarded when one of the member computers successfully solves the puzzle and creates a block. When this happens, the pool receives the cryptocurrency reward. The pool then, automatically divides the reward between the members and a part of it goes to the maintenance and the management of the pool. The amount of reward that a member gets is supposed to be proportionate to the amount of computing power that the said member contributed. The more mining power you added, the higher your reward will be.

Blockchain Fork

No cryptocurrency beginner book would be complete without talking about the blockchain fork. As discussed previously, there is not central bank or governing body that is supposed to rule over bitcoin. Because of this, no one can independently make changes in the code or in the blockchain. This is a security feature that is supposed to make the blockchain secure from tampering and fraud.

While the technology is revolutionary, it is far from flawless. As more people start participating in the mining and the use of these currencies, the flaws in the technology start to become apparent. For example, the growing size of the blockchain has been an issue with miners. With each computer holding a copy of the blockchain, the file tends to eat up a lot of storage space.

For the technology to improve and become a real currency, changed need to be implemented to the blockchain. For a change to happen in a currency system with no governing body, all the miners and nodes in the system holding a copy of the blockchain should agree. This network-wide consensus is required for a blockchain to continue a one single chain.

Most of the time however, the people in the network do not agree with the changes. With each change, there will be winners and losers. The people who are benefitting from the status quo will understandably refuse change. This results to two factions in the network.

If the number of people who wants the change implemented is big enough, they could choose to go ahead with it, even without the full consensus of the community. Those who do not agree with the change could just choose to go on mining using the old (unchanged) system.

This results to a division in the blockchain. The people who agree with the change will mine a different blockchain where the change has been implemented. Those who do not agree, will just carry on with their usual operation. This event is called a Fork.

There are two types of fork in the system:

The Hard Fork

The example discussed above is called a hard fork. It happens when the changes that need to be implemented in the blockchain requires fundamental changes in the system. These changes cannot be applied to the previous sections of the blockchain.

A hard fork can also happen if people believe that a negative event needs to be reversed. This was first observed in the case of the Ethereum DAO hacking. As a result, the Ethereum blockchain was split into two.

Bitcoin also had a number of forks applied to it to address is sustainability issue. Bitcoin Cash is an example of a fork that came from the original bitcoin blockchain.

The Soft Fork

In some cases, a soft fork can be applied to apply minor changes to the future blocks created in the blockchain. A soft fork is possible if the changes that need to be applied to the blockchain do not conflict with the previous rules of the blockchain. In this case, if everyone agrees on the soft fork, it will be applied and no splitting of the chain is necessary. The only difference is that new rules will be added to the software managing the currency. This can be applied by updating the software that the nodes use in mining.

The DAO Hack

In the starting days of Ethereum, an organization called the DAO successfully launched a crowdfunding campaign gaining more than $150 million for contributors. The amount was supposed to be used to various projects that the members of the DAO will vote to pursue. The organization will use the Ethereum network for the projects and the Ethereum Smart Contract system to handle the funds.

Smart contracts are coded instructions that are added to the blockchain. The smart contract is meant to automatically carry out the instructions after a set of conditions have been met, just like in a real contract. In the case of DAO, the smart contract has been set ahead of time. The part of the instructions in the smart contract was about how the money of the organization will be moved. The smart contract is included in the blockchain, making it public. This makes all the smart contracts in the Ethereum blockchain open to the scrutiny to the public.

It is a particularly bad idea to automate the movement of money in smart contracts. People who are well versed in coding can look at the code of a smart contract and find vulnerabilities that they can exploit to transfer Ether from an account to their own personal account.

This is the case with the DAO hacking. Many people had seen some vulnerabilities and publicly voiced them out to the DAO members. However, for some reason, the members of the DAO did not oblige to fix these vulnerabilities before the crowd funding event. This may be partly because the members of the DAO did not anticipate to receive such a big amount of money from the crowdfunding campaign.

As some people expected, an unknown hacker took advantages of the vulnerabilities of the smart contract. The person managed to siphon over 50 million dollars-worth of Ether from the DAO account. This hack had a massive effect on the Ethereum network. On one hand, the integrity of the code as the law of a decentralized currency was at stake if changes were to be applied to the blockchain. On the other, the future of the Ethereum network will be at stake because the hack affected the confidence of people who are planning to enter the network.

The Ethereum network ultimately ended up deciding on a hard fork. However, some people who did not agree to this were left on the old blockchain. The old blockchain was then called Ethereum Classic. The rest of the network applied the changes proposed in the fork and continued to use the name Ethereum. When people talk about the Ethereum blockchain today, they are referring to the new fork.

The hard fork in this case had one primary function, to prevent the hacker from withdrawing the money hacked from the DAO. Instead, a new smart contract was applied to the fund that allowed the contributors of the DAO to withdraw their money.

Chapter 3 – How do Cryptocurrencies Affect You?

The cryptocurrency market has made the news multiple times last year and people are still talking about it even after the massive rise in prices. Now that the hysteria over it has calmed down, people who are still holding cryptocurrencies are asking what will be its future.

If you are looking into participating into this market, you should also consider this question and how cryptocurrencies will affect you.

Will it become a widely-used currency?

If cryptocurrency does break out into the market to become a widely-used medium of exchange, it will become even more valuable. If this happens, there is a good chance that the price of the said cryptocurrency will surely go up.

A cryptocurrency's success however, is the problem. Once a cryptocurrency becomes popular, more people will want to buy it. This increases the demand in the market, while the supply is increasing at a slower rate each day. Applying the laws of supply and demand, this leads to a spike in the price chart.

If a cryptocurrency fixes this problem, it should integrate with other financial services online and in the real world. It may just become an alternative to cash when transacting online.

If you are hoping to become a cryptocurrency user though, it may be for some time before we actually see a real dependence on this technology in the financial industry. You will know when this is about to happen when financial services that facilitate transactions online like PayPal, Western Union and the big banks starts partnering with one cryptocurrency. At the time of the writing of this book cryptocurrencies like Ripple (XRP) and LiteCoin are already working with financial institutions to start facilitating payments between businesses. If this works, it may just pave the way for the digital currency to be used with regular consumers.

It may still take a couple of years before any cryptocurrency becomes a mainstream form of online money. For businesses to be able to use it on a regular basis, new legislations about it may need to be written, especially among the major economies around the world. Governments are wary about this new currency and its possible negative effect on their economic growth. It will take legislators time to pass bills, study the currency and actually put up rules and regulations that govern its trade and wide use.

Are you considering trading it?

As a trading asset, some governments have already placed bans on the digital currency, citing that it is being used as a money laundering tool. Traders from all over the world however, are still flocking the market. It's no longer a seller's market though. The time of massive buying of currencies has passed. Traders right now are just working with the speculative nature of the asset. When the price goes too low for Bitcoin for example, many of them buy. Because of the global nature of the trading platforms, a slight change in the price can trigger massive buyoffs or selloffs. These trader behaviors lead to the constant price changes in the most actively traded cryptocurrencies.

If you want to become trader, you will need to learn concepts like fundamental and technical analysis. Fundamental analysis is a technique in picking stocks and other investment assets that can also be applied into cryptocurrency trading. When doing fundamental analysis in stocks, you constantly look into the press releases, news, and financial reports of your target companies. You do this to establish a so-called intrinsic value for the company. You could then get the intrinsic price of a company stock by dividing the total value of the company by the total number of its issued stocks.

If an intrinsic price is calculated, the fundamental analyst then checks the market price of the company. If the market price is below the intrinsic value of the company, the fundamental analyst reads this as the company share being cheaper than it should be. Companies that have the biggest gap between the estimated intrinsic value and the prevailing market price are usually purchased.

With cryptocurrencies, instead of looking at the value of a company, you are trying to make an intelligent guess of the true value of a currency. You can do this by looking into the underlying technology and the communities managing it. For example, you could get the initial capitalization of the company who developed the technology and the amount that they got from any coin offerings they had.

You could then start looking into their progress towards the holy grail of the cryptocurrency world; to become widely accepted as real currency. A currency which has made massive leaps into becoming a major currency should increase in value. If you see a currency proactively innovating and looking for ways to become an accepted currency, then you may say that the value of that currency should increase.

Just like with picking stocks, you should also compare the said positive events and innovations of the company to its price activity. If the market price has not improved after significant progress, this may mean one of two things. First, there may be some information that you are not aware of, preventing other traders from buying the cryptocurrency. You will need to do more research about it before actually buying more of the said currency.

Second, it is also possible that people are just not responding well enough to the positive news about the currency. This could happen when the overall trading climate is bearish. This means that people are not in the mood for buying new assets. It could also happen when the cryptocurrency traders and investors are looking the other way towards a more popular cryptocurrency. All these factors could lead a currency to be undervalued or cheaper than it should be.

An undervalued currency is a great investment especially if it continues its progress in achieving the community goals. Bitcoin for example, has been undervalued for years since its inception. However, because of positive media coverage, improvements in technology and overall positive reception from the market, it managed to rise in value by over 1,000% in 2017.

This could happen again in the future but it is likely to happen with lesser known cryptocurrencies with a solid fundamental foundation.

The second skill that you will need to learn is the trading practice called technical analysis. While fundamental analysts focus on the factors surrounding the cryptocurrency, technical analysts focus mostly on the price and the market factor affecting it.

Just like regular traders, technical analysts also aim to buy when the prices are low and sell when the prices are high. However, they take it a bit further by trying to guess when a price slump will end and when an uptrend begins. They also try to guess when the price hike will stop based on the behavior of buyers in the market as reflected in the price charts.

A technical analyst bases all his or her decisions on the price movements on the charts. When the price is going down for example, they try to guess the bottom of the downtrend. They then start buying when the currency reaches a certain price.

When they already own currencies, they try to predict when an uptrend will end, which usually happens during massive selloffs. They then sell when their predicted price is reached.

Will it be outmoded because of other emerging technologies?

It is possible that other emerging technologies will overtake cryptocurrencies as the primary cash alternative in the internet. However, the likely scenario is for new technologies to be implemented as newer versions of cryptocurrencies. Banks and other financial institutions have given attention on the impact of the blockchain in the financial world and have created their own research and development teams to find possible uses for this new type of technology. It is clear that the market is in need of a decentralized currency that is not influenced by government, borders and oppressive laws. The market however, has yet to reached a verdict on which system is most suitable to become a cash alternative online.

Chapter 4 – How to Start with Cryptocurrencies

Now that you have a basic idea of how cryptocurrencies work, you should be able to make an informed decision of whether you want to participate with it or not. If you do choose to participate with cryptocurrencies, you need to learn the different roles that you can take as a cryptocurrency user:

Miner

First off, you can start your cryptocurrency journey with a mining business. To create this kind of business, all you need is the startup capital to pay for the hardware and the electricity bill. You can buy a mining rig off the internet. A mining rig is basically a computer that is made up only of slots for graphic cards. It is stripped of all computer components not needed for mining. The more graphic cards you have in your mining rig, the more computer power you will add to the network. In theory, this should increase your chances of earning money.

You will need to balance this however, with the amount of money you pay for your electricity bill. For your mining operation to work, you will need to let your hardware work 24/7. This will require you to keep them turned on all the time. The more graphic cards you have working for your mining rig, the higher the amounts of electricity it will eat up. The high electricity bills need to be taken into consideration when doing a feasibility study of whether a cryptocurrency mining operation is worth your while.

Consumer/User

You could also take the role of a cryptocurrency user. You can become a user if there is an industry for you to openly use the cryptocurrencies you obtain. As of the moment, the number of people and businesses using any cryptocurrency is still too low for them to he considered as reliable currencies.

Investor

Right now, most people participating in the cryptocurrency network are either investors or traders. Investors are the people who buy into cryptocurrencies believing that they can become successful in the future. Most investors put in a big chunk of money into the market, hoping that, over time, the value will go up. While investing in cryptocurrency certainly is an option, most players right now are just into them for short periods.

Trader

Traders on the other hand, do not put a lot of thought in the value of the cryptocurrency and its underlying technology. They are only interested on how high the prices will rise. They intend to ride the price fluctuations of these currencies to make a profit.

You can also take part in cryptocurrencies this way. However, before you go into this type of business, it is important to remember that trading is extremely risky. It is even more so for cryptocurrencies. The prices of these currencies can increase or decrease by thousands of dollars in a matter of minutes. You need to be prepared for great losses if you start investing in this market.

Service provider

Lastly, you can also take part in cryptocurrencies as a service provider. Service providers are businesses that build their business around the use of cryptocurrencies. Businesses serving cryptocurrency users are popping up around the world. Some prominent examples are cryptocurrency wallets and exchanges.

Wallets are online services that facilitate the safekeeping of cryptocurrencies. Just like a service like PayPal, wallet companies allow user to make payments and receive money.

Exchanges on the other hand, help buyers and sellers meet in a cryptocurrency trading market. They facilitate listing of currencies and provide the necessary infrastructure to help investors and traders make informed buying and selling decisions.

Many services are also built around the mining market. Computer companies for example, are selling commercially available mining rigs. There are also online services that facilitate the creation of a mining pool. Mining pools are groups of miners who contribute their computing power to work together in solving blockchain puzzles. With so many computers working together, the process becomes more efficient and the group is likely to get the reward more often. The members of the mining group then divide the loot based on the amount of hash power they contributed.

While there are a lot of services offered in the cryptocurrency related markets, there is still a lag in the services that connect cryptocurrencies with the real world. For instance, we do not see a lot of real world businesses using bitcoin or any of the popular cryptocurrency as a payment option.

Owning your first crypto coins

Now that you know what roles you can play in the cryptocurrency market, let's talk about how you can get your first coins. The process of purchasing cryptocurrency is easier than most people think. All you have to do to start is to get a cryptocurrency wallet.

There are multiple types of wallets depending on your needs. In this book, we categorize them according to where they are stored. They are also discussed in order from the wallet with the highest to the least level of security:

- Web Wallet

A web walled is hosted by cryptocurrency wallet services online. They do specialize in facilitating the transfer of cryptocurrencies and keeping them secure. Web wallets are the easiest types to wallets to start with. You could even sign up with one today. All you need is a credit card to purchase coins with.

Web wallets are run by giant for-profit companies. They are providing service for profit. They can profit in multiple ways. Some types of web wallets require a signup fee. These types of web wallets are expected to have smaller number of clients and lesser transaction fee rates.

Most web wallets though are free to sign up with but make their money from the currency spread and/or the transaction fees. Currency spread refers to the difference between the buying and selling price of cryptocurrencies. Transaction fees on the other hand are required payments for each transaction. It is usually a percentage of the total transaction amount.

Web wallets though are the most hackable form of crypto wallet. It has happened in the past and it may happen again in the future. The problem with this type of wallet is that there are multiple points of hacking vulnerability that hackers may exploit.

Hackers can look for flaws in the codes used to maintain the wallet. Because of the 100% uptime that most wallets aim for, hackers are able to continually test to penetrate the security features in the wallet code. One crack in the wall is all it takes for millions of even billions of dollars-worth of cryptocurrency to be hacked.

Aside from the underlying code of the wallet, it is also possible to for hackers to target the individual device of the users, particularly, the browsers used to access the wallet. An untrained users who does not update his or her browser or even the device operating system can be vulnerable to browser-level hacking.

The third and the more likely source of hacking vulnerability is the social factor. Web-based crypto wallets are basically multi-million dollar companies that hire hundreds to even thousands of people every year. Any of these people can be the point of attack of the hackers. Mistakes like using one's computer in a public place or accidentally talking about sensitive information in regular conversations can become actual security threats. Not to mention that the operations of giants companies like these are closely monitored by people who are in the business of hacking. A successful cryptocurrency heist can lead to multimillion dollars' worth of profits.

This is not to say that all crypto wallets are bad. In fact, it is still the recommended way of starting. However, you should make sure that the wallet company you are signing up with has a great security track record. Most experienced cryptocurrency experts would pay more in services fees in great companies than risk it with smaller, less established wallet companies.

Web wallets also tend to offer the widest access to different types of cryptocurrencies. One web wallet for example, could store account information (private and public keys) for not only bitcoin but also Ethereum, Ripple, Litecoin and other widely traded cryptocurrencies. For traders and users who use multiple cryptocurrencies, web wallets are the best storing option to begin using.

Aside from this, web wallets also tend to offer the best user interface to users. The web wallets offer dashboards to their logged in users that gives them an overall view of their different cryptocurrency accounts. These dashboards are constantly updated based on the security needs of the web application and the user experience of the user.

- Mobile Wallet

The mobile wallet is similar to the web wallet, except that the sensitive account details are stored in one's smart phone rather than in a web-connected server. This approach to storing cryptocurrency information has its own pros and cons.

Mobile wallets usually come in the form of a mobile app that can be easily installed in a smartphone. They allow users mobile access to their cryptocurrency information and, more importantly, offer security features for protecting account-specific information.

There are two types of crypto wallets that can be accessed using a smartphone. The first one is the app version of web wallets. You should not confuse these types of wallets to true mobile wallets. The app versions of web wallets are not true mobile wallets for a number of reasons. First, the information in these types of apps are not stored solely on the phone but in servers of the web wallet companies. Because of this, anyone, hackers and employees of the company, have access to this information.

True mobile wallets on the other hand, do not store account information into remote servers. Instead, they only store these types of information in the phone. This method of storing crypto account information can be advantageous from a security standpoint but may also be inconvenient to use at times.

From a security standpoint, mobile wallets are not accessible to hackers if the phone is completely disconnected from the internet. One could limit the penetration potential of the device simply by keeping its data and Wi-Fi access to a minimum. Lesser connection time means fewer opportunities for hackers.

Having a mobile wallet app also means that you are not dependent on the security of the browser. Your account information will be protected from attacks that are specifically targeted towards vulnerabilities of popular browsers like Google Chrome, Safari and Mozilla Firefox.

This form of wallet does have its downsides though. One of the most important is the fact that the quality of security of a mobile device is dependent on its make and model and the user's diligence in keeping it updated. Older smartphones tend to have a higher number of known security vulnerabilities. If you have an older smartphone, using this form of wallet, is not recommended because the operating system of your smartphone may have intrinsic flaws that cannot be fixed.

Users of mobile wallets must ensure that their devices are up-to-date, because this is the only way to make sure that the previously discovered vulnerabilities are no longer present.

There is also the possibility of losing access to information when the phone is destroyed. If the phone's memory hardware is destroyed, all files that are not backed up may be lost. A mobile wallet may offer backup options for file recovery. However, this option may lead to its own security vulnerabilities.

Changing phones frequently is common among smartphone users. The average user changes smartphones every time their telco contracts end. This presents a problem for mobile wallets that do not have backup features. Adding recovery features may also lead security loopholes.

On the other hand, the unused phone with the account data on it could also be a source of vulnerability. It is important for users to wipe the memory of old devices to make sure that it cannot be accessed by anyone else in the future. The only sure way to do this is by physically destroying the device.

The fact that mobile phones are used for multiple functions can also be a cause for concern. If you often let other people use your phone for calling, games, or the use of any other type of app, you should not use this type of wallet. Unmonitored app installations can lead to the malware infections that hackers can use as an entry point.

The storage size of the mobile phones may also become an issue. High-end phones offer multiple hundred gigabytes of ROM but this storage capacity is shared by multiple apps ranging from social media apps, news and content apps, to games and utility apps. A smartphone power user can easily fill up this storage space in a year. Reaching maximum storage can lead to the mobile wallet to malfunction. This could prevent the mobile wallet app to update. Updates usually fix vulnerabilities and bugs in the app. If they are not allowed to happen, this can lead to openings for hackers to attack.

Compared to web wallets, mobile wallets tend to offer fewer cryptocurrency options. They may offer some of the popular ones like Bitcoin, Litecoin and Ethereum but may not immediately offer newer ones. At the time of the writing of this book, these refer to cryptocurrencies like Ripple and Cardano. Adding more cryptocurrencies to the system, offer security and phone storage issues.

Mobile wallets are also run by for-profit companies. Just like the web wallet companies, they also earn through spread between buying and selling price. They may also charge access to the wallet through a one-time installation fee. This serves as a pay wall that makes the wallet exclusive to paying users.

- Desktop Wallet

A desktop wallet, offers the same features as the mobile wallet. Because desktop hardware is more robust compared to that of a mobile device, it tends to offer better cryptocurrency security features.

Just like the mobile wallet, desktop wallets are not accessible to hackers when it is not connected to the internet. A user with an adequate firewall installed and a fully updated operating system can effectively use this type of wallet.

The desktop wallet comes in the form of a software installed in the personal computer. The types of desktop wallet software available for you will depend on the operating system you use on your computer. The options of wallet software available are different for Windows compared to those for Linux.

Desktop wallets are less convenient to use compared to the other two discussed previously. For you to use this type of wallet, you will need to have access to your personal computer and the internet. Installing it to a laptop can help make your wallet more mobile.

It does however, fix some of the issues that come with the use of mobile and web wallets. Unlike the web wallet, this type of wallet stores the account information only in the desktop, allowing it to be accessed by a significantly fewer number of people. Unlike the mobile wallet, it has more storage space. If you are well-versed with computers, you can even install your wallet in a virtual server inside of your PC, to isolate it from the other software and apps installed in the device. If you have the funds, you can even give it its own hard drive with better firewall installations.

Desktop wallets also tend to have better user interface options compared to that of the mobile wallets. The better RAM and storage space available in most desktops allow desktop wallets to offer user friendly features that rival that of the web browser.

The companies who develop and maintain desktop wallet software tend to profit from the sale of their software. Because of this, the reputation of their company and their software's security features are the most important factors for them.

The downside of using this type of wallet is that it tends to be more difficult to use from a consumer standpoint. You cannot easily transact with a desktop wallet because you constantly need have access to your computer to transfer funds.

It also tends to have access to fewer types of cryptocurrencies compared to the other two types of wallets discussed above. If you want access to another cryptocurrency that is not currently served by your desktop wallet, you may need to contact the software developer to ask for it or install a different desktop wallet software.

- Hardware Wallet

The hardware wallet is probably the most radical of all the cryptocurrency wallets. It is separate hardware that contains the account information for one of your choice of cryptocurrency. Because this type of wallet is not used for any other purpose, it is expected to be safer. In a desktop wallet for example, there is still a possibility that your computer will be infected by a malware that targets your wallet software. This could still open your wallet to attacks that can lead to the theft of your money.

A hardware wallet can only be accessed if it is attached to a computer. However, because it is a standalone device, it has its own built in security features that make it safe from being infected by malware.

For these types of devices, the only way for hackers to actually steal information from it is if they had access to the physical hardware. By keeping the hardware wallet away from the reach other people, you will be able to keep its content safe.

The drawback of a hardware wallet is that it sacrifices ease of use to security. To keep it secure, you should only use it with few computers. Ideally, you should only use it in internet networks that you are familiar with. Because of this, you cannot use it when you need to constantly make buying and selling decisions fast like in the case of cryptocurrency traders.

The integrity of the hardware wallet depends on both the age of its hardware and software components. This type of wallet needs to be constantly updated to remain secure. Older types of wallets should also be replaced with new ones over time. As these devices become older, they become possible security liabilities and open to attacks. Because of these requirements, hardware wallets can become expensive to maintain.

Principles to follow to keep your cryptocurrency safe:

- Use only secured networks

As discussed above, you should not use your cryptocurrency devices and software using public networks. Ideally, you should only use them in your home or in your office or other networks where you are sure that no other people have access to. While most online wallet transactions are encrypted, they can still be sniffed from unsecured networks. Given enough time, the hackers may be able to decode the encryption. While this is unlikely to happen, it doesn't hurt to be extra careful.

It also goes without saying that you should not access your web wallet in other people's computers. Even if your friend or family member does not have intentions of stealing your money, their computers could have malware that can steal information from your web wallet. You should only use computers that you personally own and maintain.

- Keep every software in your computer or phone updated

Regardless of the type of wallet that you are using, you should make sure that you always update the software features of the device that you are using. You should make sure to constantly run a malware test on the devices where you access your cryptocurrency accounts. Use reputable anti-virus software. Ideally, you should use the ones recommended by the company that created your operating system.

Speaking of the operating system, it is the number one software that you should make sure to update. OS updates are meant to plug security holes in the computer that serve as vulnerabilities. By updating your OS constantly, you are also keeping the data in your computer safe.

Aside from your operating system, you should also keep your browser updated, especially if you use web-based wallets. Aside from the OS, hackers are constantly looking for browser vulnerabilities because it is one of the most commonly used software in the computer for accessing the internet. Make sure that your browser is up-to-date to prevent hackers from using older vulnerabilities to hack your cryptocurrency information.

- Avoid risky behavior in your computers

The computer that you use to access your cryptocurrency accounts should be free from malware and other malicious codes. Make sure to update it regularly and that you do not do tasks on it that may increase the risk of infection. This includes going to websites with questionable reputation. The most common mode of malware infection is through unauthorized downloads of files from websites. If you have not used a website before, you should research about it first before you actually visit it on the device where you access your bitcoin wallet.

If possible do not add browser extensions to your device where you access your wallet. Browser extensions can sometimes have malicious content on them. Most of the time, these content are related to spreading of online content or optimization of ad targeting. However, you can never be too sure. Just to be sure, do not install them on the device where you access your wallet.

Most importantly, you should be wary about downloading files. Files with an executable suffix (.exe extensions) are often used as the carriers of the malware. Once you double click on them, the size malware is introduced into the system and it begins spreading itself using your computing power. While most malwares can be detected immediately, some are coded specifically to do only specific actions. Some malwares though lie in wait until the conditions for their use has been met. It is difficult for anti-virus software to detect these types of malware because they are not common.

To avoid these types of malware from acquiring vital information for our computer system, do not download anything. If you see an EXE file in your computer that you are not familiar with, it is better to delete it, than double click it to see what it does.

- Only access your cryptocurrency accounts in secure locations

Also, you should not open your cryptocurrency accounts when people behind you have a vantage point of your screen. Anyone who has a view of your computer screen while you are accessing your account can take a photo of it and zoom into the details in it. It is also possible to view camera footages of the place to check the contents of your screen. If possible, only access your computer at home of in an enclosed place with no one else behind you.

- Safeguard your private key

Your private key gives you the ability to access your cryptocurrency. If people get a hold of it, they will be able to have the power to spend the amount of cryptocurrency addressed to that account.

Because of this, you should never view your private key in a public place. If you need to access it away from your home, make sure that your phone or your laptop is covered or away from the view of anyone else.

- Spread your cryptocurrencies in different wallets

The last defense against cryptocurrency hacking is the age-old adage of not putting all your eggs in one basket. If you are managing more than one type of cryptocurrency, put them in separate wallets. Remember that coin wallets are not like banks. Your money stored in them is not ensured. In case of account hacking, these companies will not pay you back.

To ensure that you do not lose your money if one of these companies make a mistake, you should not put too much of your digital currencies on just one wallet. Instead, use different types of wallets to protect your money from being taken all at once.

Chapter 5 – Most Popular Cryptocurrencies

Before you can take part in the cryptocurrency industry, you first need to learn about the different cryptocurrencies available in the market today. Since the price boom of bitcoin and other cryptocurrencies in 2013 and 2017, many copycats have emerged as ICOs.

By the first quarter of 2018, more than 45% of the ICOs that emerged in 2017 and earlier have become inactive. This is mainly because of the lack of capitalization backing them up as well as the lack of mining power that these currencies have.

For an ICO to remain relevant among miners nowadays, it can no longer take the approach that Satoshi Nakamoto took in establishing the bitcoin. The blockchain technology is no longer enough to establish credibility as a decentralized currency. Instead, it needs to establish that it is supported by a community and that it has the backing of a solid organization like major financial institutions.

Bitcoin

Bitcoin is the currently undisputed king of cryptocurrencies in terms of market capitalization and trading volume. Because it is the first one to hit the market, it has a lead over the other cryptocurrencies in terms of the number of miners in the network and price growth.

At its peak in the later days of 2017, bitcoin reached a ceiling closing price of more than $17,500. However, the spike in price experienced in 2017 was followed by a massive selloff by investors and traders. This happened in the midst of added scrutiny of different governments around the world and some even applying harsh policies towards the use and trade of cryptocurrencies. Bitcoin however, remains to be the highest valued cryptocurrency. Its closest rival, Ethereum, is still far behind in terms of market capitalization.

Bitcoin however, only leads the other cryptocurrencies in terms of being an investment asset. As of the writing of this book, it is not any closer into becoming a true cryptocurrency.

In its early days, it was used as mode of payment and a donation currency in many onion websites (websites in the dark web). With bitcoin's popularity however, many of these websites dropped it because of the increasing scrutiny of governments in the bitcoin transactions.

Bitcoin's price volatility is also one of the biggest reasons why many people are hesitant to use it as currency. No one can rely on a currency that plummets in value to over $2,000 in a matter of minutes.

With these problems still hounding bitcoin, it looks like that it will not become a cryptocurrency anytime soon. However, if you are looking for an investment asset that draws a lot of attention during peak times, this is the cryptocurrency for you.

Ethereum

Ethereum is also one of the pioneers of cryptocurrency. Unlike bitcoin which solely focuses on replacing the use of cash in the internet, Ethereum has a different approach. Ethereum aims to create platform that uses the shared computing power offered by the miners to facilitate the use of smart contracts and the development and maintenance of decentralized application (DAPPs).

DAPPs are one of the newer concepts introduced in the Ethereum system. It allows developers to create services online without the need for middlemen. Imagine of you could download your apps directly from the developer without passing through the App Store or Google Play. The only reason why we don't do that right now is because we do not know if we can trust the developer and the apps stores serve as the gatekeepers protecting our interests and taking a bit of our money in the process. With a DAPP, developers will be able to establish trust with the user using smart contracts.

Smart contracts are just like real world contracts where in there is agreement between parties. However, when a contract is encoded in the blockchain it becomes a smart contract because it cannot be altered in anyway without affecting the integrity of the entire chain.

Just like with the basic blockchain used in bitcoin, smart contracts are grouped together and arranged to create a block in a blockchain. The miners who facilitate this are then rewarded with Ether, the cryptocurrency aspect of Ethereum. Just to make this clear, Ethereum refers to the network that uses the blockchain technology to create and store smart contracts while Ether is the coins that people can exchange.

The idea behind Ethereum is for the network to have its own ecosystem where in transactions can be made and businesses can be operated. Just like people nowadays using the internet for our everyday use, the Ethereum ecosystem can also become another version of that and the Ether is the currency used inside it.

The success of Ethereum and Ether to become real cryptocurrencies largely depends on the business models of the apps that are built within its platform. As of the writing of this book however, no app has managed to breakthrough into the mainstream just yet.

Critics of Ethereum mostly attack the ambitious concept of the potential of DAPPs. The concept is still in its early days and the developers working on DAPP projects do not necessarily have a blueprint to follow. Instead, they are the trailblazers of this new form of technology.

One reason why the DAPP is difficult to develop is the fact that the code of the smart contract needs to be foolproof because it cannot be changed. Once the smart contract is set, there is no way to stop it from executing its function when the right conditions are met. This can be dangerous if the code of the contract is vulnerable to attack. It is particularly dangerous if the smart contract is designed to handle the transfer of money.

Ripple

Ripple is a relatively new cryptocurrency but it has made a big impact in the industry in the short time that it has been here. It became a massive hit since its ICO. However, it also slumped in the major selloff in the beginning of 2018.

Ripple is the first currency to partner with banks and major financial institutions. This is its main selling point right off the bat. Its founding company, a company called Ripple Lab, is continuing to develop the network so that it fits seamlessly with some of its financial institution partners which include The Royal Bank of Canada and Standard Charters. It has also partnered with money transfer giant Western Union to research on blockchain applications in the money transfer business.

Ripple is made up of two important parts. The Ripple system also called RippleNet is the payment network. It is the connection between banks and other financial institutions that are participating in the network. The second part is the cryptocurrency called, Ripple XRP. This is the currency used to represent fiat currency in the network. When XRP is transferred from one node in the system to another, it is understood that an equivalent amount of fiat currency is transferred.

For a time, Ripple was second to Bitcoin in market capitalization. This happened in the later part of 2017. The massive increase in price increased the value of Ripple, giving more research and development capital to its development company.

Ripple's main goal is to use the blockchain technology with financial institutions to make global transactions faster. A transaction that crosses borders usually takes multiple days. The banks currently use the SWIFT system for authenticating transactions. This system usually requires 3-7 banking days to process. Other blockchain technologies have made this method faster but Ripple stepped it up a notch. Processing a transaction with Bitcoin for example requires just over an hour. Ethereum can process the same transaction in two minutes. A transaction in Ripple can be completely processed in just 4 seconds.

Unlike Ethereum, Ripple really focuses on the financial world. In fact, Ripple refers to itself as a payment platform rather than just another cryptocurrency. The success of Ripple largely depends on its ability to transition into the business world. As of the writing of this book, it is one of the closest cryptocurrency or blockchain-based technology to penetrate the financial market together with Litecoin.

However, Ripple also has its critics. Some cryptocurrency purists do not think that Ripple is a real cryptocurrency. Many of them believe that, because its system is intertwined with the workings of the banking system, it can never be truly decentralized. This does not matter to the developers however, because they never really set out with the goal of replacing cash. Instead, they merely want to improve an outdated banking and money transferring system.

Bitcoin Cash

Bitcoin Cash usually stands in fourth place in terms of market capitalization. Bitcoin Cash was created as a fork from Bitcoin as a response to the scalability issue of the original cryptocurrency.

Ever since the beginning, Bitcoin has been criticized for its limit in the size of its blocks. The bitcoin blocks are limited to only 1MB. This would mean that the number of transactions in a block will be limited. In the beginning, the value of bitcoin was low. At those values, more bitcoin could be sent out in each transaction. Nowadays, the value of bitcoin has reached so high that people are now sending minute amounts of bitcoin. With its popularity, the number of bitcoin transactions increased. As more transactions wait in line, many of them experience delays. For some, it could take more than an hour for a transaction to be processed.

Many members of the community believed that changing the size of the blocks is the best strategy to this problem. This is the proposal that many thought made sense. In August of 2017, a large chunk of the community implemented the Bitcoin Cash proposal, giving birth to the hard fork version of Bitcoin. The main feature of bitcoin cash is the changing of the size of the block from the original 1MB to 8MB per block.

As an independent cryptocurrency, bitcoin cash has stood on its own for more than 5 months now as of the writing of this book. Its price reached a peak of more than $4,000 in the boom of 2017. However, it did not keep this price and it dropped back down, hovering around the $1,100 to $1,300 range.

Its main selling point is that it uses the same hashing function as bitcoin. Because of this, bitcoin miners can easily transition from mining bitcoin to mining bitcoin cash.

Since Bitcoin cash is still too young, it is impossible to say if it is here to stay. Many cryptocurrencies forked from the original bitcoin blockchain in the past but most of them did not get enough number of miners and developers to keep their currencies alive. Bitcoin Cash seems to be the first Fork of bitcoin to successful stand.

Litecoin

Litecoin is also one of the pioneering cryptocurrencies that followed bitcoin. It has been coined by many as the silver to bitcoin's gold. It was released just after bitcoin, with one major difference, its hashing algorithm. While bitcoin uses the SHA-256, Litecoin uses Scrypt.

The difference in the hashing algorithm has many effects that aim to address the shortcomings of bitcoin. One such effect is faster block generation and generally faster transactions. The blocks in Litecoin are bigger and can be generated using simple computers like personal computers with a number of GPU cards.

Bitcoin's reliance on SHA-256 has led to the so-called arms race in the mining community. Miners have been look for ways to increase raw computing power through the use of specialized mining rigs. Using these rigs is not necessary with litecoin. Instead, it opens up the possibility of mining through the use of high-quality personal computers.

The growth in Litecoin's value pretty much followed that of Bitcoin. When Bitcoin peaked in price back in 2013, Litecoin's value also increased. From hovering just over $2 the previous months, its price soared to more than $40 in the later days of 2013.

The coin was relatively quiet between 2014 and 2016. Its priced at this timeframe hovered around $1 to $8. It began to pick up again in the early part of 2017. It peaked in price and trading volume in December of 2017, reaching more than $350. Since then, Litecoin continued to flourish with prices between $150 and $300 per coin. The strong showing following the market crash came in the wake of multiple positive news about the coin. In particular, it was the subject of interest of multiple banking and money transfer institutions for blockchain research in the financial industry. Just like Ripple, it is one of those cryptocurrencies that is being considered as a true replacement for cash in the internet.

Cardano

Cardano is the fifth largest cryptocurrency in terms of market capitalization as of the writing of this book. Just like bitcoin, it aims to be a cryptocurrency however it has multiple changes in the application of the blockchain technology.

The main feature of Cardano revolves around its structure and its unique programming language. It uses a programming language called Haskell, which is said to be robust and flexible. The choice of the unique programming language is said to be a solution to the ever-changing landscape of the cryptocurrency market.

Using this programming language, the developers developed a multilayered blockchain system. Just like bitcoin and other cryptocurrencies, it has blockchain dedicated to organizing and documenting the transactions made. It uses the proof of stake algorithm.

The second layer of cardano is another blockchain where in the reason for transferring funds is documented and organized. This is an attempt to make the smart contract concept better, by separating the management of money from the other details of the contract.

While Ripple is built with the needs of the financial institutions in mind, Cardano on the other hand is focused on balancing the privacy and decentralized features of a cryptocurrency to the need to regulate it. It has identified that the lack of a proper regulating features is preventing governments and financial institutions from accepting cryptocurrencies in their respective countries. A solution to this is a smarter smart contract and multiple layers of protection that are absent from its predecessors.

The developers boast that Cardano's code and structure is based on academic research and peer-reviewed publications. While its features may seem to answer many of bitcoin's shortcomings, its late entry to the market is preventing it from reaching its full potential in terms of pricing.

Cardano's success will depend on the technological development projects that its team develops to convince other cryptocurrency users to transfer from the use of other currencies. As of the moment, currencies like Litecoin and Ripple are more popular the Cardano. When being compared to other cryptocurrencies, it is still no clear what the underlying technology offers that this new to the market. Until Cardano can establish integration with the financial world and the benefits of using it in contrast to other cryptocurrencies, people will have no reason to transfer to Cardano.

Cardano's price peak in 2017 was around $1.30. It plummeted back to below $1 per coin in the wake of the massive selloff in 2018. It remains to be seen what the future holds for Cardano. Currently, its bets of both worlds approach does not motivate people enough to transfer to it.

Chapter 6 – How to Trade Cryptocurrencies

To start a trading a cryptocurrency, you should first learn the basics of investment. You need to learn how to find investments assets with good fundamentals and those that are just hype jobs.

A hyped investment asset may seem like a solid investment it you only consider its face value. However, the often truth comes out about its true value to society. Their value tends to suffer when this happens.

One of the problems with investing with an investment asset like cryptocurrencies is the sheer amount of investing that happens. Cryptocurrency investing is derived from Forex or Foreign Exchange investing. To trade successfully with any currency, you need to choose a pair that is commonly traded.

Understanding currency pairs

A currency pair states the relationship between two types of currency. Each currency in a pair is usually represented by a three-letter symbol. Bitcoin for example, is represented by the BTC symbol. Each currency should have a unique symbol so that there will be no confusion in the trading market.

A currency pair is then represented by two currency symbols joined by a hyphen. As of the writing of this book, the Bitcoin to US dollar currency pair is the most commonly traded in the market. This pair is represented by BTC-USD. Each currency pair has a corresponding price or exchange rate.

The BTC-USD for example has reached the price of $19,870.62. This means that 1 bitcoin was worth that much US dollars. The price of the currency varies and it changes almost every minute as the trading of the currency pair continues.

Because the BTC-USD pair is the most commonly traded in most markets, it is easy to find. However, some exchanges may operate with different currency pairs. An exchange in Japan for example, is likely to offer BTC-JPY for the Japanese Yen. In the same way, Chinese-focused exchanges are likely to offer BTC-CNY for the Chinese Yuan Renminbi.

Cryptocurrency Exchanges

In the wake of the 2017 price boom, many cryptocurrency exchanges opened for business. Exchanges are private businesses that facilitate the exchange of cryptocurrencies between traders. To assist in the trade, the exchange must provide the traders with a secure online environment where they could freely exchange their money. Some of the features of good exchanges are:

- High number of traders

One of the keys to the success of an exchange is the number of people using it. The more people trading it an exchange, the more accurate the pricing of the currency pairs will be for that exchange. Traders however, tend to pick the exchanges that are most beneficial to them. If an exchange for example, does not have the currency pair that they would like to deals with, they are likely to find another one that does.

The number of traders reflects the liquidity of an exchange. With more traders in the market, it will be easier for you to find buyers and sellers. On the other hand, an exchange with relatively fewer traders is difficult to work with. It is common for traders to have the same state of mind. This happens when traders get the same set of news and market data. They tend to act in the same way.

Conditions like a homogenous trading environment and too few traders lead to bad trading conditions.

- A wide range of cryptocurrency-to-fiat currency pairs

Next to the exchange's popularity, you should also check if they offer trades in the currency pairs that you would like to trade with. The biggest currencies do have a wide range of currencies to choose from. The smaller ones though, only deal with specific currencies.

As of the moment, Bitcoin is the most popular cryptocurrency. Because of this, most exchanges have bitcoin paired with whatever fiat currency they use as their operational currency.

However, before you do sign up with an exchange, it is important that you find another cryptocurrency to trade in other than bitcoin. If you are just starting out, try to learn about how the other biggest coins like Litecoin, Ethereum and Ripple work.

While it is not necessary to trade with all of them, you should try to keep up with how other currencies are doing, what improvements are being made and what the projected future is for these currencies. More importantly, you should also make yourself aware of the currency exchanges that do offer pairings to the currencies you keep track of. Knowing which exchange to go to will help you in acting fast when you find actionable information about a currency that you are not familiar with.

- Low transaction fees

The investment gains that you get from your trading activities do not represent your net income from the exchange. With each transaction you make (buying and selling), you pay a transaction fee. Part of the transaction fee goes to the people who make the transaction possible (miners). However, the exchange may place their own service fee on top of it. This is how cryptocurrency exchanges make money. They charge for the service they offered every time a trader buys or sells.

When you are looking for an exchange to start trading with, you must look up how their transaction fees compare to the others in the market. While the transaction fees may seem small, they tend to add up as your trading activity increases. It is also a rule of thumb to only deal with exchanges with a completely transparent statement of fees. In each transaction you make, it should be clear how much of the money goes to the miners and how much of it goes to the exchange. Make sure that you are aware of these factors before you pull the trigger with one currency exchange.

- Multiple cash-in and withdrawal options

Cashing into and withdrawing from the exchange should be easy. The exchange you choose should have the option to buy in using non-credit card options like PayPal and other online services. Adding one extra layer between the exchange and your financial information will significantly help in deterring hackers from targeting you.

It should be also able to connect to your preferred coin wallet. Coin wallets are generally more secure than cryptocurrency exchanges. However, some people choose to keep their money in their exchange wallets for convenience purposes. You should avoid doing this, especially as your cryptocurrency portfolio grows. Instead, look for exchanges that can easily move your funds from your third-party coin wallet to keep your money safe when you are no longer trading.

It should also be easy to take your money out of the exchange. When you have turned your cryptocurrency back into the US dollar, your money should be easier to move. You should be able to withdraw it with ease back to your coin wallet or your preferred money merchant.

If you find reviews that withdrawals with a certain currency exchange takes too long, you should avoid that crypto exchange.

- A user-friendly user interface

One of the first things that you will see when you sign up with an exchange is their dashboard and the trading user interface. These parts of the trading platform are usually featured in the instructional videos of the cryptocurrencies as well as in the tutorials and knowledgebase of the exchange. Ideally, you should spend some time tinkering with the user interface of your chosen exchange before you do an actual trade. Become familiar with your tool first, before you risk your money.

- Fair pricing of cryptocurrencies

The pricing of cryptocurrencies varies for each exchange. However, the differences between the pricing should be almost the same because the exchange base their price on the transactions added to the blockchain.

However, some exchanges consider other factors when computing the prices of currencies. Some for example, add the factor of the difference between the number of buyers and sellers in the market.

When choosing a cryptocurrency market, make sure that you check how the prices of their major coins compare to other exchanges. These prices are usually shown even to nonmembers. Avoid exchanges whose prices of currency pairs are too far from the pack.

- A track record of stability and security

Most of the exchanges you see online are not regulated by any government. Investors need to have a certain level of trust in these exchanges to start investing.

To find a trustworthy exchange, make sure to check past news about them. In particular, you want to look for news about hacking and other events that may have led to investors losing money outside of their trading activity. If there is such an even in the history of the exchange, try to find out how the exchange responded to it.

If possible, you should only deal with exchanges that never had these events in the past. This is the best way to ensure that your personal information will be safe with them.

Most successful cryptocurrency exchanges:

BitFinex

As of the writing of this book, BitFinex has the largest market share of all the cryptocurrency exchanges. It boasts an average 24-hour trading volume exceeding $1.2 billion. The closest one on this list has an average trading volume of $900,000.

For the majority of 2017, the majority of the trading volume in BitFinex comes from the BTC/USD pair. However, as of the writing of this book, the ETH/USD pair has significantly closed the gap. If you are looking into trading in these cryptocurrencies, you should certainly open an account here. Aside from these two, they have one of the widest selections of cryptocurrency listing. They offer the biggest names in cryptocurrency and some of the less popular ones.

You could find their website in this URL: https://www.bitfinex.com/

CoinOne

CoinOne is an exchange with mostly South Korean users. However, it is still included in this list because it second only to BitFinex in the market share of exchanges. The operational currency for this exchange is the Korean Won (KRW). Just like with other exchanges, this was dominated by the BTC pairing in the majority of 2017. The BTC/KRW pairing dominated more than 90% of the trade volume in CoinOne in that year.

However, unlike in other exchanges, the perception of the market in CoinOne can rapidly shift, depending on the prevailing cryptocurrency news among Korean traders. As of the writing of the book, the Ripple XRP/KRW pairing is the most dominant pair in the exchange.

While South Korea may seem like a small country, its traders are actually some of the biggest drivers of cryptocurrency prices in the world. Their preference to trade with XRP for example, drove the price of the cryptocurrency to more than 20% in less than two weeks.

You can access CoinOne in their official website: https://coinone.co.kr/

Kraken

Kraken holds the third place in the cryptocurrency exchange market share. Its defining feature is its Euro pairs with some of the biggest cryptocurrencies. As of the writing of this book, Kraken's trade volume is split between the BTC/USD, BTC/EUR, XRP/USD and ETH/USD.

However, it also gives you the option to trade with less popular cryptocurrencies like Litecoin, Cardano and Ethereum Classic. All these cryptocurrencies are available in USD and EUR pairings.

You can access the Kraken signup website here: https://www.kraken.com/

BitStamp

BitStamp closely follows Kraken in the market share list of cryptocurrency exchanges. This exchange is based in the United Kingdom. However, the pairs with the highest trading volume are BTC/USD, XRP/USD and ETH/USD. They also offer Euro as an alternative operational currency and they also list Litecoin as an option for trading.

You can access the BitStamp website and sign up for an account in this URL: https://www.bitstamp.net/

Coinbase GDAX

Coinbase GDAX is the exchange version of the most popular bitcoin wallet. The exchange's operational currency is the US dollar and its most popular pairs are with BTC, LTC, BCH (Bitcoin Cash) and ETH.

If you already have a Coinbase web wallet, it is only logical to use this exchange. However, many of the big names in the cryptocurrency market are missing in their listing. If you are looking to trade with XRP for example, you may need to find another exchange because Coinbase GDAX does not have it in their listing, as of the writing of this book.

Trading Strategies

Just the same principles are involved with trading cryptocurrencies as with other forms of trading. All you have to do is to remember to buy low and sell high.

The only thing different with cryptocurrency is the fact that the price is extremely volatile compared to other forms of assets. Any investor needs to adjust his or her trading strategies based in this unique factor.

Make sure you are up to the challenge

Before you buy your first cryptocurrency for trading, you should make sure that you are aware with the unique market conditions that surround this type of trading. Unlike other trading assets, with cryptocurrency, you will barely have any time to adjust. You need to be constantly reviewing information about the market and making buying of selling decisions.

If you are used to buying and holding assets, the cryptocurrency trading world may not be for you. As stated above, the prices of assets in this market change constantly. If you fail to pay attention to the market just for a few minutes within the day, you may end up losing hundreds of thousands to even millions of dollars.

Operate big

Because of the high transaction fees and the constant price fluctuations, you can only make a lot of money trading if you work with large sums of money. If you have good actionable information, you should cash in on it by backing your decision with large sums of money.

If you only operate with a small amount of money, it will take you some time to increase your portfolio size. By operating with a large amount, you will minimize the impact of the fees involved in trading.

Trade short when the market is booming

The spread of herd mentality is great with cryptocurrency. Cryptocurrency trading is the new buzzword in the investment world. When news about it spreads, it spreads fast. This is particularly true about news of prices increases for a particular currency. When there are massive gains with a particular currency, the news media immediately picks up on it and reports about it. When big news outlets begin to spread the news, the other smaller publications also begin to pick it up. Some may even stretch the truth based on the original publications.

Because of the way media works right now, the news about novelty investments like these spread fast. This affects the public and investor perception of the market. When they see positive news about a currency, many of them who have money to spare begin to consider taking part in it. They begin to feel like they are missing out from the massive gains of the cryptocurrency market. Many of these people do not even know what cryptocurrencies really are aside from the shallow Google search they made prior to deciding to participate in the market.

What's unique about the cryptocurrency market is that it is open for trading to billions of people around the world. Anyone with a credit card and connection to the internet can start dealing in cryptocurrency. Due to this unique borderless trading setup, anyone who hears about the news of a certain cryptocurrency can easily take part in the market.

This makes cryptocurrency markets open to massive and fast price fluctuations. When prices increase by 30% and up daily, which is unheard of with any other type of asset, you could expect that the growth is artificial and unsustainable. In short, there is a bubble in the market. An economic bubble happens when the price increase is only based on asset market demand. When people just buy bitcoin for example to make profit, you can expect that all of them with this kind of goal will end up selling their positions soon enough. They are not willing to stay in the market to actually use the currency. The moment they see a sign that the price increase is about to end, they will bail on the market and try to sell as much of their coins as possible to take their own profit.

In the 2017 cryptocurrency boom, banks and financial institutions around the world were still wary about the market. However, in some places, especially here in the US, hedge funds with short positions on bitcoins and other cryptocurrencies began to appear. You could expect more of them to come out when the market begins to become popular again, just like what happened in 2017. When this happens, find an institution where you can take a short position with. If you can establish your short positions in a booming cryptocurrency at the right time, you will be able to make a lot of money.

Diversify as your portfolio grows

Cryptocurrencies are one of the best types of assets to trade with when you are just starting out. By trading with cryptocurrencies, you will be able to get massive rates of return that are unheard of in other types of assets.

As you grow your portfolio size however, you should start to translate your digital earnings to real world businesses and investments. Right now, the cryptocurrency market is at its infancy and no one knows which one of the many currencies in the market will stay for good. Each of them are constantly growing and evolving to fit the needs of the market. However, it is inevitable that one will be favored over the others.

You do not want to be heavily invested in any currency once the crypto-mania has passed. Instead, you want to start relocating your assets to other businesses and investments so that you can translate them into real monetary gains.

Do fundamental analysis of all cryptocurrencies you trade with

Cryptocurrencies are like products. The more people participate in their trade and the more people use them, the higher their value become. Before you pull the trigger to buy one type of cryptocurrency, make sure that you do the necessary research on it.

First and foremost, you should look into the people or company who developed these cryptocurrencies. The industry today, with few laws regulating its use and trade, is riddled with illegal activities. One of the trending illegal schemes is the pump and dump scheme. These pump and dump schemes rely on making their ICOs look as legitimate as possible.

When you are in the hunt for a new cryptocurrency to buy into, make sure to research the people behind it and the goals of the developers for creating it. Try to learn the motivations of these people and if they are ready to support the development of their ICO in the long haul.

Pump and dump schemes do not always involve fake coins. Sometimes, the people who operate these schemes also use legitimate currencies. Their goals, is basically to create an artificial demand for a particular currency through hard selling tactics. They use profiling techniques to target people who are most vulnerable to it.

The best way to avoid these types of schemes is by doing your due diligence on researching about the currency. It is highly suggested to look into the company that offered the ICO. You should make sure that the cryptocurrency they offer is decentralized, meaning that they do not have total control over its management and in the changes in its rules.

It is also better if the company or group that started the ICO has a publicly announced leader or spokesperson. This gives you and other traders a person to ask questions from when things go wrong. The words that the leaders of these companies say in public make them accountable for possible crimes.

It also helps if you stick only to those currencies that are already established but still has room to grow. You will know if a company is still open for growth when there are still a lot of coins to be mined. For bitcoin for example, there are still just under 20% of coins to be mined as of the writing of this book. As the number of coins left to be mined decreases, it is also expected that the price of the coins will rise because the number of coins that can be created is fewer. It is also expected that the price of the coins will increase when the reward for mining is split into two in June of 2020.

The same principle should apply to other up and coming cryptocurrencies. In the beginning, when their following (number of miners and coin owners) is low, the value will remain low. As the number of currencies in the market, begin to increase exponentially through mining in the early days, the value will remain to be low. However, most of the profits will be earned when the news about the value of the cryptocurrency begins to pick up. This can happen in a variety of ways depending on the type and featured of the cryptocurrency. When it does happen however, we may see the same price patterns similar to what happened with bitcoin in 2017.

However, you should also consider that the price boom may not happen at all for some of the new currencies, particularly it if is not marketed well. You should also expect that the market will not necessarily react to the news of a new ICO in the same way as they did in the previous year. With the public becoming more familiar with what ICOs are and what cryptocurrencies are for, they will be less reactive with hype news about new currencies.

Because of this, it is important to evaluate each new cryptocurrency for the additional value and features that they add to the market. If a new currency is no different from bitcoin or Ethereum, then you should not expect it to become valuable in the future because the needs that it covers are already covered by its predecessors.

Bet on the cryptocurrency that is likely to become real money

As of the moment, there is no cryptocurrency that is likely to break into the mainstream fiat currency market. This is partly because many of these cryptocurrencies still have fundamental issues that make them unreliable as a true currency. Issues such as the volatility of the price, the illegal use of the currency and the long transaction periods should be fixed first, before the currency can become a reliable replacement for real world money.

Becoming a widely used currency is the Holy Grail among the currencies in the market right now. The cryptocurrencies that were released later like Cardano and Ripple, tried to make adjustments in the implementation of the blockchain technology to address these issues. However, for the time being, none of them seem to have cracked the code for becoming a real replacement for money.

When looking into an ICO, check if its defining characteristic solves some of the important problems discussed in this book. If its features are able to solve these problems, they may just have a chance to become a widely accepted currency.

Look into the participation of institutional investors in the Crypto Market

In 2017, we saw the investing world take a crack at cryptocurrency trading. However, it is worth noting that not a lot of institutional investors publicly claimed that they took part in the currency trading. While traders play with the short term price fluctuations in the cryptocurrency market, institutional investors continue to stay away from the investment.

The reason for this is partly because of the speculative nature of cryptocurrency trading. As far as investment risks go, cryptocurrency trading is one of the riskiest assets in the market today. The high level of risk was demonstrated in January of 2018, when the peak price of more than $19,000 per bitcoin plummeted to below $10,000. Evens like these happen because the price of the asset does not have a real world bearing that the market can base a true fundamental analysis on.

It is expected that institutional investors are looking for cryptocurrencies that may be able to solve this issue. If institutional investors to take part in the market, we can expect the value of some of these cryptocurrencies to increase. The investing activities of these types of investors are regulated by the laws of the countries where they operate. In short, they can only invest on the types of assets that are aligned with the investing principles they presented to their investors. As long as fundamental issues exist in the currencies in the market, you can expect these types of investors to stay away from them.

Time your entry in the market

As discussed earlier in the book, the prices of cryptocurrencies peaked back in 2013. At the time, bitcoin and some cryptocurrencies that were based on its code were the only ones in the market. It was the first time that Bitcoin cracked the $1,000-mark.

After the price came back down however, it was a long time before the price spiked again. It wasn't until 2017, four years after, that the price of bitcoin and the other new currencies in the market rose to new heights. If you were already following bitcoins and other cryptocurrencies back then, you would have hand around 4 years to accumulate bitcoin and the other currencies before its price ballooned.

These days, people aren't buying into the market yet. The effects of the massive selloff in the early part of 2018 are still fresh in their minds. However, this does not mean that there will not be another peak coming. It could happen tomorrow, next year or five years from now. With all the news surrounding cryptocurrencies however, the massive rise in the prices is bound to happen.

The best way to trade right now is to accumulate coins with diversification in mind. If you currently have a monthly savings of $1,000 for example, allocate a part of it to your investment portfolio. After that, decide on how much money you will send towards your cryptocurrency portfolio.

When investing in them, it is better to go straight to the exchanges yourself and do not go through the investment funds offering cryptocurrency investments. If there are investment funds investing in cryptocurrencies in your country, you should expect that they will have bigger than usual management fees and transaction rates.

Instead of going through these funds, start your own account with cryptocurrency exchanges and do the buying and selling yourself. As stated previously in this chapter, these accounts are user-friendly enough to be used by beginners. Make sure though to consult the knowledgebase and the tutorials offered by the exchange management to learn about all the features that you can enjoy with the account.

Use Index Investing Principles on Picking Currencies

In terms of what currency to buy, you should not go around buying them blindly. You should keep track of the news about cryptocurrencies in the market and base you decision on which currencies are active. When the market starts to explode again, the ones that are constantly on the news with positive reports are the most likely to rise in price. The obscure ones will get the least of the attention of the market participants. This will result to a slower increase in price in times when the cryptocurrency market is bullish.

You could also apply the basics of the index fund investing principles to cryptocurrency. In this method, you only buy currencies that fit a certain set of criteria. For example, you could choose to buy only the top five cryptocurrencies based on their market capitalization. The amount of money that you should put into a specific cryptocurrency should depend on the weight of that cryptocurrency in the market.

Let's say that the top five cryptocurrencies in your list has a combined worth of $350 billion dollars and the top cryptocurrency in this list has a total of $192 market capitalization. This means that this particular currency holds 54% of the total capitalization. When following the practices of maintaining an index fund, you can also invest 54% of your money to that cryptocurrency. You could then adjust the weight of investment on each currency by adding or removing funds every two weeks.

By using this method, your portfolio size will grow based on the average growth of the top currencies in the market. It also takes away the speculating part of the process. In this method, the currency-picking technique is almost automatic.

Picking the top currencies also has other benefits. One of the most important is that, these currencies are the most liquid in the market. They reached a high level of capitalization because of the market activity. When the price starts rising again, they are the ones that are most likely to increase in value.

When the cryptocurrency market is idle with minor price fluctuations, that's the time when you should start buying. The price fluctuations that we see right now is nothing compared to what can happen in the future. However, we do not know which of the currencies will have the biggest growth. In the past decade, it has been bitcoin that took the lead. However, as more people learn about cryptocurrencies, there is a good chance that other currencies will also start to gain some traction and have their own massive price increase.

By positioning your portfolio in all top five or even top ten cryptocurrencies, you are increasing the chance that you will get a piece of the growth of both the established currencies and those that are just starting out but have a good chance of growing.

Quit while you are ahead

Before you invest in cryptocurrencies, you should set a goal of how much you want to get out of the market. When the market is starting to become extremely bullish, that's the time when you should start thinking of selling. In the past, we've seen that the cryptocurrencies are capable of appreciating by more than 1,000% of its original value. However, there is no need for you to reach these levels before you should pull your money out. Instead, you should base your selling decision on your personal goals.

After accumulating currencies in the low points of the cryptocurrency market, you should have a balanced portfolio made up of the top cryptocurrencies in the market. When the market starts becoming hyperactive again, the prices of these cryptocurrencies should start to increase. When this happens, you will get closer into reaching your goal.

The decision on when to sell your cryptocurrency assets is a crucial part that will decide how much profit you will get. When wild price growths happen like the ones that happened back in 2013 and 2017, the smarter people in the market are always thinking of when they should sell their assets off. The idea is to sell before the rest of the market participants do. If you manage to sell at the peak of the price spike, you will be able to make maximum profit. However, it is impossible to know when the peak price will come. This is why you should aim to sell off nearest to the peak price. If you manage to sell off your assets between 80% and 99% of the peak price, you should already consider that a successful trade.

Buying longer term versus day-trading

Many beginners are drawn to the practice of day trading. The purpose of this trading strategy is to maximize the principle of buying low and selling high to the point of doing it multiple times every day. However, for you to be successful in doing this, you need to be right in the majority of your trading decisions. The most experienced investors in of the assets markets will tell you that no one is right all the time. Even the best of traders who use both the fundamental and technical analysis techniques are not always right.

Even if you do make a profit with day trading in cryptocurrency, it is likely that it will all be cancelled out by the transaction fees of the trades. Each transaction you make will generate this kind of fee and the day trading model requires you to make between 3-5 transactions every day.

Instead of trying to make pennies with day-trading, aim for long term growth with your cryptocurrency investments. As suggested in the previous tips, you should be able to accumulate a lot of coins when the market is not getting a lot of press. At this time, only the most loyal of traders stick around in the market. The majority of people do not want to participate in it. Many of them choose to participate when they see that the market is in an uptrend.

By buying when the market is down, you increase your chances of getting coins at a cheap price. If you see that the price of coins is cheaper the following week or month, you should buy some more. Do not doubt that the market will rebound in the future.

When the prices of bitcoin plummeted in 2014, critics were fast to point out that it is a worthless asset. These critics, however, were nowhere to be found when the prices rose again in 2017. When the prices fell again in 2018, people started doubting cryptocurrencies again. This cycle will continue throughout the development of the blockchain and cryptocurrencies in general.

Instead of listening to these critics, you should instead focus on building your portfolio when the cryptocurrencies are priced low. You should then begin to sell them off when the price peaks again.

Chapter 7 – Why is the Price so Volatile

When you start investing in cryptocurrency, you will see that it is one of the most volatile assets in the investment market. As mentioned before, its price can vary by thousands of dollars from one day to the next. In this chapter, we will talk about why this is the case and how you should respond to it.

Cryptocurrency versus fiat currency

The best way to understand cryptocurrencies is by comparing it with the money we know and love, also known as fiat currencies. Fiat currencies or regular money is the agreed upon medium of exchange in a certain country. In the United States for example, we have the US Dollar while Mexico and Canada have the Mexican Peso and the Canadian Dollar respectively.

These fiat currencies are just paper money, coins or digital numbers on a screen. However, they are respected as a tool for facilitating trade of goods and resources because of a number of reasons. The first one is because all the people in a certain location agree of its value and its legality.

The second reason why fiat currencies are widely accepted is because its value is stable. If you see a brand new car that you like to be worth $20,000 today, it is likely to still be at that price by tomorrow. In reality, any business can price their products or services with any amount they want. Women's handbags for example can be worth a few bucks to multiple thousands of dollars. Business owners and manager though, are limited by market factors that require them to make reasonable pricing decisions. Because of this, most of the commodities we see in the market are priced somewhat fairly, based on the market supply and demand.

Part of the reason why fiat currencies have stable values is because they are managed by the central bank of a country. Here in the US, we have the Federal Reserve System policing the use and trade of the US dollar. Each country has its own version of a central bank.

The central bank is constantly in a balancing act to make sure that the growth of a country's economy is manageable. To make sure that negative economic conditions like recessions and economic bubbles, don't happen the central bank tries to police all the financial institutions. It also creates and manages policies that are aligned with the goals of the central government to boost the growth of the market.

With currencies, the central bank is in charge of creating and destroying paper money. Too much printed money in the circulation can lead to inflation or the rising of the prices of the goods and services in an economy. The central bank can lessen the inflation by managing the number of printed currencies in circulation.

The central bank also has the power to set the interest rates that banks are allowed to impose to their borrowers. This affects the ability of businesses to grow. When the interest rates imposed by the central bank are low, it drives businesses to borrow more money to be used for growing their business. They borrow more in this condition because the price of borrowing money, the interest rates, is low. They can easily pay for both the borrowed money and the corresponding interest rates with their profits.

When the interest rates are high however, businesses cannot easily borrow money because the price of borrowing is high. It will take a bigger chunk of their profits to pay off the principal amount ant the corresponding interest of the debt.

In a low interest rate economic environment, economic growth is expected. The economy is likely to grow because there is more cash in circulation. The success of businesses in making profits trickles down to employees.

However, this type of economic conditions may also be inflationary. As more people are able to afford the goods and services in the market, the prices of these goods and services also increase. If too much of this is happening, the central bank may increase the interest rates to slow down the economy.

The value of a fiat currency is affected by the skill of the central bankers to balance the growth of the economy. In reality, fiat currency values are determined by market activities also known as supply and demand. If the economy of a country is doing well relative to the performance of the economies of other countries, more foreign investors will want to invest in that country. When this happens, the currency of a country is in high demand. The investors who want in will need to exchange their currencies to the fiat currency of the country they want to invest in.

When more people want a certain fiat currency, it becomes stronger. If a currency becomes stronger for instance, it will take more US Dollars to buy one unit of it.

Now, you may be asking how this is related to cryptocurrencies. The answer lies in one of the fundamental features of a cryptocurrency, in that it is not managed by any central bank and that its value is not tied to the value of the economy of any country. Because of this, the values of cryptocurrencies are only dependent on the supply and demand in the market. No one can print more of it instantly and no one can destroy it when there is too much cash in the market.

In the past couple of years that multiple cryptocurrencies have been publicly traded, the lack of a managing body led to massive fluctuations in the market price. It is common for Bitcoin, the most popular cryptocurrency, to jump in value by a few thousands of dollars per unit. When good news about a cryptocurrency hits the market, the number of buyers also increases leading to a spike in the price.

The social media culture

The internet and culture of social media is one of the biggest driving forces in the buying and selling of cryptocurrencies. When people see that the people they know are profiting from a certain asset, they feel that they also want to take part in it. Not everyone gives in to this urge. However, this Fear of Missing Out or FOMO drives people towards the cryptocurrency market.

This is particularly true for traders from other asset market. A stock trader who isn't doing well with his practice in the stock market for example, could choose to transfer some of his funds to trading bitcoin. Some people whose lifesavings are just sitting in the bank begin to get idea of putting a part or all of it in the cryptocurrency market to increase its value. The collective actions of people who go into the market increases the price of the assets listed in it and this is primarily driven by what people hear in the news.

The same is true when people are thinking about buying out. When people are already in the market, they are always thinking of when they should buy out. They are afraid of pulling their money out prematurely because they do not want to miss out on possible profits. However, the smart investors and traders understand that each minute longer that they spend in the market increases their risk of losing a big chunk of their profits. To balance the risk and the rewards out, these people depend on the news that they get in the media. They keep track of the information about the cryptocurrency market and the changes that may possibly affect the price.

The news about these markets differs each day and each one is constantly devoured by the traders and the people who are planning to participate. When a particular news story that paints a positive light about cryptocurrencies start spreading, people start to buy cryptocurrencies. A small spike in the price of bitcoin for example will generate a lot of positive news about the market. This in turn will make people think that the market is doing well again, prompting them to start buying up assets again. The positive effects of this in the price will continue to feed the system until the peak is reached.

In regular asset markets like the stock or the commodities market, the price increase usually stops when the market has reached a saturation point. This is the phenomenon when the majority of the traders and the investors have already spent the most of the funds that they are willing to put into the market. When this point has been reached, short-term traders begin to initiate their profit taking strategies. This results in the massive selloff in the market which drives the prices down.

At times, the saturation point does not need to be met for a price uptrend to stop. The price uptrend could stop abruptly when bad press about the market starts to spread. In the 2018 cryptocurrency selloff, the price went down right after news about tightening government policies around the world. In particular, it was the policies in the East Asian and South East Asian countries that triggered the event. South Korea, one of the most active cryptocurrency trading countries, was one of those countries. The South Korean government decided to close down local cryptocurrency exchanges that were reportedly involved in money laundering schemes. They also imposed policies that required cryptocurrency account holders to attach their exchange accounts with their bank accounts.

While the policies in South Korea may seem like a limiting factor in the trade of currencies, they were nothing compared to the policies imposed by the Chinese government. China banned all cryptocurrency trading altogether by closing all local exchanges and blocking access to the websites of international exchanges.

Needless to say, all the news about the policies that aimed to control, and even stop, cryptocurrency trading led to the great selloff of 2018. With this in mind, you should always keep track of all the news in the market whenever you are holding cryptocurrencies for the short term. When you read about or new negative stories about the cryptocurrency you are trading with, ask yourself how wide the story will spread and how it will affect the perception of the market.

This brings us the next factor that affects volatility:

The actions of traders

Though this book does not recommend day trading to its readers, there is no denying that there are some people who do last long doing this profession. Traders are masters in their techniques of being ahead of the people getting the news and predicting the behaviors of people in the market.

Cryptocurrency trading has evolved to become one of the most active trading markets in world. The market capitalization of many cryptocurrencies dwarf market capitalizations of many companies around the world. In a span of a day, billions of dollars-worth of bitcoins and Ether is moved. Many of the movements come from traders who are looking for intra-day profits within the market.

The hourly transactions of these traders create the daily fluctuations in the market. Even after the days following the massive selloff in January and February of 2018, the market was extremely active. People who were fearful of more losses wanted to dispose of their coins. On the other hand, people with a bullish mindset in this time, bought the massive amounts of coins entering the market at extremely low prices. In the months that followed, people continued to actively trade bitcoin on a daily basis. Some of them are medium and longer term-minded investors who are planning to stay in the market for the long haul, aiming to ride on the next great price increase. The majority however, are short term buyers and sellers who are focused on the daily fluctuations in the market.

The activities of these individual traders will continue to make the price of the biggest coins fluctuate on an hourly basis. You should not allow these price variations however, to distract you from your own strategy and goals. Instead, you should focus on building your coin portfolio.

The activities of the traders in the market may appear to affect the prices of cryptocurrencies in a big way right now. But in the future, many of these cryptocurrencies will be valued even bigger as more participants start investing in the market. When the smaller cap currencies like Ripple or Cardano increase in price in a similar way that bitcoin and Ethereum did, their current price movements may seem insignificant. This possible price increase will happen when the mentality of the investing market turns from bearish to bullish. A bearish mentality is not looking to buy coins. After a great selloff like the ones that happened in 2014 and in 2018, people begin to have a bearish mentality. They do not want to buy cryptocurrencies thereby pulling the prices down. When the memory of the great selloff disappears and positive news about cryptocurrencies begin to flood the airways, that's the time when the market perception begins to shift from bearish to bullish.

A bullish mentality refers to the collective perception that the market is doing well and will continue to do well. This mentality reflects on the behaviors of the traders and the newcomers in the market. Experienced traders use technical analysis of the price to try to guess when this will start to happen. They aim to increase their ownership of a cryptocurrency just before this happens. Their collective actions of buying cryptocurrencies together with the buying actions of the newcomers in the market boost the price to unprecedented levels.

Lack of an intrinsic value

One of the primary reasons why cryptocurrency prices fluctuate so much is because of its lack of real world value. Fiat currencies have developed over time. In the ancient times, currencies were created from precious metals like gold and silver. Almost all civilizations at the time agreed that these precious metals have great value because of their unique appearance and rarity. Because of this, kings did not hesitate to use gold and silver as their material of choice for coins. Merchants willingly obliged in using these metal coins as a medium of exchange because of their universal value. If a kingdom falls, its coins do not necessarily lose all its value because they can still be used in other kingdoms that also view gold and silver as valuable metals. In the worst of cases, a merchant can simply have the gold or silver coins melted and formed into jewelry to be sold for a profit.

For a long period, precious metals had been used as the material for currencies. However, some people accumulated a large amount of gold and silver that they can no longer store them all in their pockets and even in their own homes. To cater to this need, banks were created to store the gold, silver and other precious metals. A bank will provided a safe place for people to keep their coins and in exchange, they gave the people what we now refer to as bank notes. Bank notes started out as pieces of paper, indicating the amount of coins a person had in the bank. When they transact, they simply gave a few pieces of these notes to the people they transacted with and those people can have the note exchanged for real coins in the bank. This is basically how cash transactions were born. People in a civilization agreed that the notes they were holding were just as valuable as the coins they had stored in the bank.

Eventually, people were so accustomed to using paper money or cash that they simply did not care about gold and silver. However, even in the early parts of the twentieth century, our civilization did not completely abandon the use gold and silver. For a very long time, the value of cash was based on the amount of gold that a country had. This is what we refer to as the gold standards. The US implemented this system at around 1879. The Federal Reserve continued to use the gold standard up to 1933.

Nowadays, the value of cash is completely based on the economy of its source country and the economic policies of its government. When the economy of one country is booming and its policies are beneficial to foreign investors, more people will want to buy its currency so that they can transact and invest in the economy of the said country. This increases the demand for the currency of this particular country. An increase in demand results to an increase in the price of the currency.

Let's take the US dollar for example. When the economy is booming, more people want to come to the US because of the opportunities that our country offers. These new people coming in, needs to exchange the currency they had from their home country into the US dollars. The collective demand for the dollar results to a price increase.

However, when the economy is not doing well, investors want to leave and find opportunities elsewhere. Investors in the country will try to exchange their dollars for the next country they will invest in. If there is a massive amount of people selling their dollars in the market, the price of the dollar will decrease.

However, both the central government and the central bank work together to make sure that the price fluctuation of the currency does not become extreme. When the price of the dollar is becoming too high for example, the central has the option to print more money. An increase in the supply of cash in circulation tends to have a negative effect on the value of that currency.

On the other hand, if there is a massive decrease in the price of the dollar, the central government can create stimulus packages like giving money to the poor. This in turn, leads to increased economic activity that may just lead to investors coming into the country.

There are many other factors that may affect the price of a currency. The point is that the government and the central bank have the power to adjust economic policies to prevent the fluctuations for becoming extreme.

Now let's turn our attention to bitcoin and the other cryptocurrencies. One of the primary features of these currencies is that they are decentralized. This means that there is no one regulating body that has the power to change the policies that governs the cryptocurrency. The only way for changes to be applied is if all the players in the market agree on the proposed changes. With millions of people taking part in the market, it is almost impossible to get 100% consensus.

Because of the difficulty to implement changes in the policies that govern cryptocurrencies, no one person or group can influence the value of their value. This is at least true for the most widely traded currencies.

With the forces of supply and demand applied to these currencies and the lack of a governing body to regulate its use and management, there is no one who can stop the massive fluctuations in prices. When experts say that the value of a cryptocurrency will triple in the next five years, these claims are within the realm of possibilities. However, it is also a possibility for a currency's value to go down by more than 50% in a matter of days or weeks. We have seen this happen with many currencies in the massive crypto selloff in the early part of 2018.

The inflation rate of the source country of your operational fiat currency

Inflation rates in a country affect the spending power of its fiat currency. If the US for example, is experiencing high inflation rate, this will result to a decrease in value of the US dollar. If the US dollar decreases in value, you will need to spend more of it to buy cryptocurrencies. Unfortunately, the value of the US dollar or any fiat currency is also volatile. Though it is not as volatile as the prices of cryptocurrencies, it can fluctuate enough on a daily basis to affect the cryptocurrency-to-fiat currency pairing price.

The best way to prevent this factor from negatively affecting your portfolio is by avoiding buying cryptocurrency at times when the inflation rate is high. During these times, you will need to spend more of your fiat currency to buy cryptocurrency. It's smarter to wait for your currency's value to increase before you start buying cryptocurrencies.

It is also advisable to avoid exchanging between fiat currencies to trade in the cryptocurrency market. Let's say your credit card is in Euro. You should only deal with exchanges that use Euro as its operational currency. You do not need to exchange your Euros for US Dollars. Exchanging between two fiat currencies opens your investment funds to additional risks.

Chapter 8 – The Dark Side of the Cryptocurrency Market

The world of asset trading can be very addictive. When serial traders see a new type of asset becoming popular, it tends to awaken their curiosities. Most of these serial traders do not want to miss on an opportunity. Their ego and their wealth depend on making the profitable decisions.

In the past it was the stock market that took the attention of these serial traders. After a while, the speculative nature of the Foreign Exchange Trade took most of their attention. Now, the newest financial asset in the market is bitcoin and the other cryptocurrencies.

The massive influx of traders in the market brought about the significant price increase in the price if cryptocurrencies last year. Many of these traders to do not come into the market, hoping that the price will go up. Many of them have plans on how to drive prices. In January of 2017, when the price of bitcoin was just picking up, governments around the world weren't concerned about it yet. Because of this, there was little to no regulation happening in the buying and selling of cryptocurrency. With no laws governing its trade, it brought the attention of many traders with mischievous ideas.

Fake ICOs

In 2017, there were countless illegal schemes surrounding the different cryptocurrencies. One of the most common schemes used was setting up a fake ICO. Telemarketers called multiple would-be investors inviting them to invest in new cryptocurrencies that would double in value within a year. Many people saw that this was not impossible in the case of bitcoin and

Ethereum. As a result, many people unwittingly fell for such schemes.

As an investor or a cryptocurrency user, you should make sure to only deal with the most popular cryptocurrencies to start with. Do not go on venturing the newer ICOs yet. These scammers are good at what they do. They will set up a convincing front to convince you and other people that their ICOs are legitimate. They may have a website with all the necessary information about their so-called currency. However, at the end of the day, all these tools for validation end up to be smoke and mirrors.

Make sure that you check with reputable financial sources like Investopedia or Yahoo Finance before you give your financial information to initial coin offerings. By doing your due diligence, you will be able to avoid scams like these.

Credit Card Scams

In many cases in the past year, people have fallen for a trick that would not ever work in the real world. The scheme goes like this. A person or a group of people pose as legitimate businesses online, looking to buy bitcoin or any other popular cryptocurrencies.

They will find willing buyers who are willing to let go of some of their bitcoin. These scammers will have some tricks to make their act seem believable. Instead of buying all your bitcoin for instance, they will ask if they could only buy half because they are short on cash. Or they may offer to exchange it for another type of cryptocurrency before agreeing that they pay you with cash.

They do all this to convince you that they are legitimate buyers who are just inexperienced in the matter of dealing with cryptocurrencies. In the end, they will agree on transaction and they will give you a credit card number with a valid pin to validate. Thinking that the deal is done, you or any other person who wants to make a profit from his or her cryptocurrencies sends the currency over to the buyer. After a week or so, the transaction with the credit card is flagged. The bank transaction is reversed because the credit card has been reported stolen. The information provided by the buyer is false. While the real credit card owner gets his or her money back, you on the other hand have no means of getting back your cryptocurrency. That is just the nature of a cryptocurrency. It is anonymous and it cannot be reversed unless both parties agree to do it.

With no name to present, there will not even be a case filed because the identity of the thief is never found.

Pump and Dump Schemes

Aside from the two illegal schemes presented above, the stock trading trick of pumping and dumping is also rampant in the cryptocurrency market. If you are unfamiliar with this scheme, it usually starts with a fake ICO or even a legitimate one. The important factor is that it needs to be cheap so that many people can afford it.

After picking the ICO, the organized crime group pools their money to put it all in their target currency. After pumping the currency full of money, its value begins to rise. The group then activates the second part of the plan, which is to put the telemarketers in their payroll into action. These telemarketers sell the cryptocurrency as if it is the next bitcoin. They sell hard and fast, moving from one call to another until they get the sale. They promise everything to the person they are calling, pushing them to put all the cash they could come up with into the market.

When the price of currency has reached its peak, the members of the organized crime group start to pull out their own money from the network. They then take the profit, abandoning all the people they duped into buying the currency.

While they are pulling their cash out of the market, they keep their telemarketers active, telling their investors to stay on the market because the losses are just temporary. This will ensure that the members of the crime group have enough time to liquidate their own assets. At this point, the people who are left late in the market are the ones who will lose the most money.

Money Laundering

Not all crimes in the cryptocurrency market have victims. Sometimes, this market is merely used by bad people to clean up their cash. Cash acquired through illegitimate methods is hard to spend. If the government sees that a person who has no declared occupation is spending millions of dollars, it begins to become suspicious.

To avoid the scrutiny of the law, criminals need to be crafty in the way they move their money. In the past, they had to work with dirty bankers, lawyers and even politicians to move their money and make them legitimate.

Now, however, they have a new method of moving their money without the government noticing through cryptocurrency. Long before cryptocurrency became a hit in the investment world, it was already a widely used method of exchange in the criminal underworld. Websites in the dark web all accept cryptocurrencies to keep the identities of the website users anonymous.

Chapter 9 – The Current State of the Market

Cryptocurrency is currently in its infancy. While it may seem like so many things have happened since the price boom of 2017, don't think that the currencies we see in the market today are in their maturity. Just like any form of technology, cryptocurrencies and the blockchain technology will continue to develop. The money that these digital currencies accumulated on their Initial Coin Offerings (ICO) will continue to fund research and development. More tools and supporting infrastructure will be developed to make cryptocurrencies a legitimate replacement for cash online.

The Near Future

In the coming year, cryptocurrencies will continue to be traded like it is being traded today. Bitcoin will still continue to lead the market. However, currencies with smaller market caps have the biggest potential of becoming big. In particular, the market is beginning to prefer currencies that are backed by legitimate companies and supported by public personalities. XRP for example, is on its way to another price increase, maybe recovering some of the value it had in 2017.

We will see more price increases like we did in 2017. When prices begin to peak again, we can expect traders from different countries to flock to the market. The herd mentality will continue to bring prices up, even beyond the previous ceiling prices.

The next price boom could be triggered by a number of reasons:

Positive Government Policies

In the middle of the 2017 trading frenzy, governments needed to act fast to protect their citizens from the dangers posed by cryptocurrency trading. This resulted to some shortsighted policies that brought about the great selloff in the early parts of 2018.

However, banks and other financial institutions are trying to learn new ways on using the blockchain technology in their operations. If the pioneering banks find positive applications of this technology, there is no doubt that other smaller banks will follow their lead. As a result, these other banks will consult with cryptocurrency developers and on how to use the blockchain in their operation.

The participation of banks and other financial institutions in cryptocurrency research will help cryptocurrency's case with governments around the world. The major cryptocurrency breakthroughs in the financial industry may happen late in 2018 or in 2019. However, there is no guarantee that this will happen.

Integration with other Industries

News regarding the success of use cases of cryptocurrencies will bring about increases in their prices. As of the moment, only the investment industry and the financial sector are motivated to use cryptocurrency. However, researchers in various academic fields are looking into the other applications of blockchain.

Among the cryptocurrencies, Ethereum has the best chance to branch out of the investment market and the financial industry. Its DAPP concept is attracting developers from around the world, thereby increasing the value of Ether. However, in the thousands of DAPPs that will be created, more than 90% of them will fail. This has been true in the website creation and App creation industries in the past and it is expected to have the same outcome with Ethereum DAPPs.

The questions will be if the top 10% of the DAPPs developed will be enough to attract consumer support to the Ethereum network. This will depend on the types of apps that will be developed.

Increased Usage Rate Outside as actual Currencies

Cryptocurrencies have thrived as financial assets. In fact, this is its only important function right now. If just one of the many cryptocurrencies in the market can break through as a currency, it will boost the value of other cryptocurrencies in the market and the other promising ICOs that will come out in the future.

As stated in previous chapters, only a few of the cryptocurrencies have actual chances to become real currencies. Many experts believe that this can still happen when a specific industry embraces a cryptocurrency as their primary medium of exchange. Bitcoin for example, was embraced by dark web websites as their medium of exchange.

The more likely industries to embrace cryptocurrency as a medium for exchange are those that deal with digital products. These types of products and services are not entirely tied to materials in the real world. Content products for example, like audiobooks, videos and downloadable software, do not require real world materials in their product. They can be instantly sold and delivered to the user who in turn can use cryptocurrency as a payment method.

Some researchers are also looking into the application of blockchain as an antipiracy tool. Digital products purchased can be logged into a blockchain with specific identification numbers. This identification code could then be used to verify people's ownership of these digital products.

Aside from the tech industry, researchers are exploring other applications for the cryptocurrency and blockchain technology. Some are looking into using it as a global record for land registration while others are looking into its application in the fields of education, sales and many other industries.

The Distant Future

There is no denying that cryptocurrency's future is still unclear. For them to become successful in the long run, their declared use cases must first be realized. Bitcoin's primary use case for example is to replace cash as the primary medium of payment in the internet. Bitcoin's success depends on whether it will achieve this use case or not. If it does not come to fruition, it is still possible that bitcoin will continue to become an investment asset. However, if people begin to believe that the primary use case of a currency is unattainable, there is no doubt that the currency will begin to lose relevance. This, in turn, will lead to the depreciation of its price.

If you do choose to take part in the cryptocurrency market, it is important that you keep yourself aware of the news regarding the development of the cryptocurrencies that you are participating in. Also, in the process of picking the currencies to take part in, make sure that you choose the ones with the best chance of succeeding in achieving their use cases.

Conclusion

The cryptocurrency market and overall industry are dynamic. New news stories and developments come out every day. If you wish to become a participant in this market or industry, you should keep yourself up-to-date.

While governments and cautious investors may be wary with cryptocurrencies, there is no doubt that it is a revolutionary form of technology. There is no limit to the use cases of the blockchain. However, it will take some time for us to realize its true value.

The only sure thing about cryptocurrencies is that the research and development efforts will continue. More funds will go into developing new technologies to build on what we already know. People will continue to support the already implemented currencies right now as investment assets. However, this will not be a smooth ride. There will be many losers in the rise and fall of cryptocurrency prices. However, the smart one who put a lot of thought into their investing decisions will come out on top.

It is also in the nature of cryptocurrencies to attract personalities with illegal intents. This is the primary reason why there is intense government scrutiny in the technology. If you do take part in the trading of these currencies, make sure that you keep track on the different policies applied by governments to their use and trade. While some currencies may have a negative impact on the market, they will become precedents to future laws that will make the cryptocurrency industry better.

After reading this book, try to reflect on the importance of this new technology and how you wish to take part in it. The cryptocurrency and the blockchain technology are developing. As they develop, they will open up new career and business opportunities. By keeping yourself aware with what's happening in the market and in the development of the technology, you may be able to find your niche in the market and make a living. You may even be able to help develop this new technology to be a force of good in the society.

I wish you the best of luck!

To your success,

William Seals

www.ingramcontent.com/pod-product-compliance
Lightning Source LLC
Chambersburg PA
CBHW020452220526
45464CB00002B/961